THE
3D
WORKPLACE

MAKING
WORK
WORK
BETTER

LASCELLES & MAGUIRE

INFLOW
PRESS

*To my wife Kate for her unwavering love,
support and editing. My rock.*

James

*To my wife Emma and son Bertie. Together we make my most
treasured three dimensional team.*

Rob

Contributors to The 3D Workplace

The authors would like to acknowledge and thank the following contributors to The 3D Workplace for their stories, examples and development of the approach.

Andy Hopkins

Anu Khanwalkar

Ben Monks

Caroline Couch

Ed Tregurtha

Fabian Schulz

Harry Workman

Ian Thornton

James Roberts

Jody Coleman

Joel Toms

Josh Elliott

Katy Mirzaie

Laurent Lemberger

Matt Jones

Oli Barnett

Sam Thornton

Simon Tarbett

Sophie Cooke

Verity Rose

Contents

Foreword by Simon Elias

Since the creation of the Lean Competency System in 2005 at the Lean Enterprise Research Centre (LERC), Cardiff University, I've had the opportunity to observe first-hand many organisations' efforts to implement continuous improvement (CI) and create a sustainable CI culture. When it comes to making the case for this change, it's been clear that most business managers readily appreciate the logic of 'going lean' – after all, who wouldn't want to embrace the notion of enhancing customer value, understanding demand, removing waste, improving quality, optimising the flow of productive activities, while fostering an engaged and empowered workforce of problem solvers?

However, the challenge many face is identifying precisely when and where to start, what to concentrate on and figuring out the right methods and tools to use that suit their particular circumstances. Consequently, many never get round to starting, and some that do, only do it half-heartedly or use an inappropriate approach that has little impact or no sustainability – and indeed, can even result in condemning CI to the sidelines for years.

Thus the need for clarity of direction and correct method selection has never been greater and this is where *The 3D Workplace* offers particular value for the manager committed to implementing CI, as it offers a highly accessible, well grounded, pragmatic, practical and flexible guide to implementing and sustaining CI in the workplace.

There are other important implementation lessons that have been learned. First, the importance of clarity and simplicity in learning communication, so that the message actually gets across, is understood and can be acted upon; second, the need for an holistic and eclectic approach to CI, so that the practitioner avoids following a too narrow path that can end up in him or her using 'one tool to solve every problem'; and third, the need for a strong focus on people and teams, as a powerful collective ethos and positive individual engagement are widely acknowledged to be critical to embedding and sustaining a lean culture.

The 3D Workplace 'ticks these boxes' admirably. It's readable and relatable, with a rich vein of cases and anecdotes running through it, based on James and Rob's extensive experience which lends it a high degree of credibility. It's cleverly labelled and the checklist approach provides a very helpful route map to follow and ensures that no stone is left unturned.

The 3D 'method' is well anchored in established underlying CI principles and importantly draws upon a wide range of CI-oriented thinking, allowing practitioners to adopt a 'contingent' (…it depends…) approach to implementation. At the same time, it ensures the manager addresses questions in critical areas, such as customer value and demand, capacity management, measures, teams, staff capability development, sustainability and engagement. Importantly, it also acknowledges that there are different ways to get started.

Finally, a major strength of this book is that it is based on what has actually worked in a wide range of organisations, through experimentation and numerous implementations. This means its readers can be confident about the replicability of its modus operandi and that it can lead to positive results and have real impact.

Managers invariably need a powerful stimulus to set them on their CI journey – to apply knowledge in the workplace and build capability through 'learning by doing' – and *The 3D Workplace* provides this 'call to action' in admirable style.

Simon Elias

Director – The Lean Competency System

Cardiff 2022

Thanks and acknowledgements

The 3D framework, called 3D from now on, has been developed over the last five years by James, Rob and our colleagues. It is a common-sense approach to making work work better.

For the purposes of this book, we refer to James and Rob as 'I'. We have worked together for many years and that keeps it simple. 3D is updated on an annual basis. This book is based on version five. The updates include improvements to existing methods plus new tools and technologies as they become available. Agile, remote working and intelligent automation are recent examples. 3D provides a common-sense business framework to incorporate these innovations. This means they stay part of the whole and not separate initiatives.

A special thanks to the core 3D development team, many of whom have contributed their own stories and examples to this book. These colleagues have led its development and continuous improvement over the last five years.

Our biggest thanks go to the many organisations who have chosen to use 3D to benefit their customers, people and bottom line. These organisations have adapted and refined the approach for their environment. Integrating 3D into how they do change. Creating their own brands that resonate with their culture.

Part One
INTRODUCTION

Simplicity is the ultimate sophistication

- Leonardo da Vinci

The goal of this book

The goal of this book is to help you make your work work better. I've spent the last twenty years working with organisations to do this. This book is based on that experience. It's not a book of theory. It's a book of practicality, stories and action.

I've five main observations from my experience to date.

1. There's a big opportunity. Many work environments do not work particularly well for one reason or another. Naturally, this is a constant source of stress and frustration to the people working in them. We want work to work well. We want to add value – as much value as possible. We want happy customers. We want recognition and praise.

2. A need to share the basic principles more widely. While the principles of work working well are familiar to people who specialise in the subject, they are not generally well known. It's not a standard topic that is taught in schools and universities except as a specialist subject. Often with quite daunting names such as Operational Excellence or Total Quality Management. This is a pity as these principles are simple to learn, easy to implement and make a big difference fast.

3. It's more fun when work works well. We've all experienced that inner glow of a job really well done. When everything went without a hitch. When our customers were delighted and told us so. When the actions and outcomes just seemed to flow. When frustrating and recurring problems finally got fixed and work became fun again. I use the word fun deliberately. Let's face it, most of us spend the majority of our lives working. Isn't it important to enjoy it as much as possible?

4. People welcome positive change. The saying *'people resist change'* is a half-truth. It needs to be extended to *'people resist change when they perceive it as negative and threatening. People welcome change when they perceive it as positive and enhancing.'* I've worked with thousands of people using the principles in this book over the past twenty years. Once people have the time and training to absorb them then they embrace and share them with their colleagues. The vast majority of people welcome adding more value, being more creative and having more fun.

5. The people who do the work are the people who know how to make it work better. I sometimes hear comments like 'our people don't have the skills/knowledge/know-how/enthusiasm (take your pick) to improve things.' I've found just the opposite. The people who do the work absolutely know how to make it work better. What's missing is the framework to channel their expertise and enthusiasm into actionable change. One proviso: it's important that the people can choose how to use and adapt the framework to their needs. Having this choice builds ownership and engagement.

So really the goal of this book is bigger than just making your work work better. It's to make your whole work environment work better. For you, your colleagues, your organisation and your customers.

About this book

This is a book of stories. For me, stories make things real. They are from experiences over two decades. I have used artistic licence where similar points have come from two or more experiences; these have sometimes been combined into one story to avoid duplication. For this reason, the stories do not relate to any particular organisation. Some stories are about situations that have gone wrong. I personally learn more from failure than success. The purpose of this book is to share both what works and what doesn't work. *Stories, examples, quotes and definitions are highlighted in a black italic font.*

A few principles I've followed in writing this book. There's no jargon or consultant speak. It's all plain English. I use the 'eighty/twenty' principle covering the essential twenty per cent of methods and tools that deliver eighty per cent of the result. Once you get going with these twenty per cent you'll have the foundation in place and the momentum to pick up the rest as needed. There's no fancy PowerPoint. It's not necessary. Examples and illustrations are all hand drawn. Everything in this book can be accomplished with a whiteboard or a flip chart, some Post-it notes and a bunch of Sharpie pens. And reasonably neat and tidy handwriting! Finally, I frequently share my viewpoints with comments like: many organisations do this, or such and such is typical. These comments are my personal viewpoints based on what I've seen, discovered and experienced in my work.

I've tried to stay at fifty thousand feet and avoid getting lost in the weeds of a particular tool or method. This is designed to be a fast and easy read. The good news is that additional detail and templates are available at **the3dworkplace.com**. Just sign up and download them for free.

Use this book like a Spanish tapas menu. You don't have to wade through a three-course meal at the local bistro. Instead just choose exactly what you want: 'I'll have the gambas al ajillo, croquetas de jamon and pan con tumaca please.' Read the next section: **What is 3D?** and then just dive in and digest the items that you want.

Finally, a special word about remote working. This book has been written on the basis that teams and people are working together in physical proximity. That keeps things simple and helps explain the underlying concepts and principles. The good news is that all the main points and methods can also be achieved in a remote working environment. So for example, where I have referred to a physical whiteboard this could just as easily be a virtual Zoom or Microsoft Teams whiteboard. There is a white paper in **the3dworkplace. com** on how to use 3D in a remote working environment.

Who is this book for?

This book is for people who are not satisfied with their current work environment AND want to do something about it. This is an important 'AND'. It's easy to moan, complain, blame someone else, point the finger. But don't! Leave that for your competitors. You and your colleagues want to do something about it. This book gives you a fast, simple and hands-on way to make it happen.

Does the actual type of work and environment matter? Not that much. This book includes examples from small, medium and large organisations. Private and public sectors. Service and asset-based. Profit and non-profit. The same principles apply.

Here are some examples of people and organisations that have and are successfully using the principles in this book to transform their work environment and day-to-day working experience. They are in no particular order and are included to demonstrate the wide variety in terms of size, sector and type of work. You'll find the stories behind many of these examples in the book.

- A trading company wanting to move to a place where, in the words of the COO: 'Not everything has to be a project to get improved.'

- A Michelin two-star country hotel renowned for its food and service ensuring that that every issue is known and dealt with immediately – including getting to the root of the problem.

- A global bank needing to transform its commercial lending

process into a brilliant client experience, twice as fast and at thirty per cent less cost.

- A start-up agriculture services company of fourteen people, fed up with the constant waste and rework, wanting to have a standard, more effective way of working together.

- A major government department urgently needing to improve ways of working in teams and between teams as it moves to a remote working environment due to COVID-19.

- A fast-growing management consultancy needing to transform its recruitment process from average to brilliant in terms of candidate experience, speed and quality of hiring.

- A retail energy company of tens of thousands of people wanting to – in the words of the CEO – 'completely change the way people approach their work'.

- A premium beverages company needing to streamline twenty of its core processes such as taking orders through to receiving the cash to realise the benefits of a new global IT system.

- A legal insurance company needing to revolutionise its product line, customer experience and cost base to grow market share and increase profitability.

- A major provider of renewable hydropower energy looking to optimise the daily operation of their network of rivers and dams.

- A sports retailer needing to urgently improve how its teams on the shop floor work as a team and with other teams.

- A manufacturer of aircraft engines wanting to embed and sustain a culture of continuous improvement.

- An individual striving to improve his ways of working to stop doing unproductive things and just concentrate on the high value and enjoyable stuff. (OK hands up. That's me! I'm always looking for new and better ways to apply the principles in this book to my own life.)

These examples and stories all have one thing in common. They involve a group of expert and enthusiastic people wanting to make things work better. 3D provides the framework to convert their expertise and passion into a stream of actionable improvements.

Part Two
WHAT IS 3D?

The right question is usually more important
than the right answer

- Plato

Background

I've tried and used every improvement method that I could find. It's been a journey of learning, mistakes and innovation. Along the journey three themes have emerged that work well both in themselves and in how they support each other.

1. How teams work. Theme one is improving the way teams and individuals work. A key point is that these improvements are within the gift of the team and the individual. They are not dependent on someone or something else. This is important and empowering for the teams and the people concerned. It is something that they can change right away, that costs nothing (or next to nothing) and that has immediate impact. It is the basis for change in the daily working culture and for individual skills development.

2. How processes flow. Theme two is improving the way processes flow across the organisation, its geographies and functions to deliver value to customers. Both external and internal customers. Ultimately, the success of any organisation is going to depend in large part on the effectiveness and smooth running of its processes. How well they work directly impacts customers, staff and operating objectives.

3. How culture supports. Theme three is sustainability. There is a force of natural decay and deterioration that over time turns order into disorder. This is neither good nor bad. It just is. The article *'Entropy: Why Life Always Seems to Get More Complicated'* by James Clear puts it well: *'It is the natural tendency of things to lose* *order. Left to its own devices, life will always become less structured. Sandcastles get washed away. Weeds overtake gardens. Ancient ruins crumble. Cars begin to rust. People gradually age. With enough time, even mountains erode and their precise edges become rounded. The inevitable trend is that things become less organised. This is known as the Second Law of Thermodynamics. It is one of the foundational concepts of chemistry and it is one of the fundamental laws of our universe.'* (Clear, J. 2020)[1]

This means that any improvement initiative that is going to become part of culture needs a continual focus on sustainability as part of itself. Not as an afterthought or when the boat starts to tip over. I often say to clients: 'By the time you need to focus on sustainability, it's too late!'

My colleagues and I developed an approach that brings these three themes together into an improvement framework called 3D. The three dimensions are:

- **Team by Team**
- **End to End**
- **Again and Again**

Team by Team means we empower our teams to self-organise how they work in a really smart way. End to End means we streamline our processes to better serve our customers. Again and Again means we keep it going for the long run. It's just the way we do things around here. From this point on, I refer to the three dimensions by their shortened abbreviations: TBT, E2E and AAA.

The rest of this book is sharing the 3D way of working with you. I hope you find it helpful and that it makes a real difference to you, your customers, colleagues and organisation.

3D Five Questions Checklists

3D uses a Five Questions Checklist for deploying each dimension. Just follow the checklists and get going right away.

All the material in this book relates back to one or more of the checklist questions. Answering these questions is where the rubber hits the road. They are designed to unlock the expertise and passion of everyone involved and focus them into a stream of practical change and improvement.

Their power lies in asking the right questions to the right people in the right order. You do not need to have the perfect answer. It is an iterative process. The main thing is to get the first iteration underway. The rest will follow. Sometimes analysis is needed part way through answering a question. Good! That means we are finding out something that we should know but we don't know. Whether it takes hours, days or weeks per checklist – so what? The point is that you are underway and you will see and feel the change immediately.

The checklist questions have a common theme. They enable a group of passionate people to engage in a structured discussion to arrive at solutions to fix problems or simply to improve things. There is only one thing required to make these checklists work for your organisation. That is to actually follow them. There's only one prerequisite. And that is to realise that there is no prerequisite!

Grounded in Lean thinking

3D is an improvement framework that combines the best of many different methods. At the same time, it is firmly grounded in Lean thinking.

1. What is Lean thinking?

My definition of Lean thinking – and there are many – is: *Lean is flowing more value to customers for less resource by the elimination of waste.* Short and simple. Every word counts. Let's look under the hood.

Lean. This definition of Lean is an improvement philosophy and applies at every scale, from the very large to the very small. The very large might include how the various elements of an organisation work together to grow the business. The very small might include how a service engineer organises the spare parts in their van. This holistic view of Lean is the subject of a paper that I wrote in 2016 called *'A Fractal View of Lean – or why Broccoli is good for you!'*. (Lascelles, J. 2016)[2]

Flowing. Flow is a powerful word. It conjures up images of streams and rivers. Artists enter a state of flow when they create. What interrupts the flow of a river? Lakes, pools, eddies and back currents. Dams, silt and mud. It's the same with processes. The lakes are piles of inventory. Eddies and back currents are rework. Silt and mud are waste.

More value to our customers. Lean puts the customer at the centre. The only purpose of a team or process is to flow value to customer(s). What do our customers actually value? We may assume we know. Often we don't. So let's ask them. Let's go and watch them in action. It might be great design, reliability, price, speed of service, an easy transaction. Note the (s) at the end of customer(s). Most teams and processes have more than one type of customer. Agreeing who are the different types of customers and how we prioritise them is key to any improvement initiative.

For less resource. Time, money, people effort, materials, mineral resources, trees, water, air, carbon: these are all resources. How can we use less of them for the same result or better?

By the elimination of waste. Eliminating waste never ends. There is always more waste to find. Just like cleaning a really messy room. It's only when we have set the furniture straight and had a good chuck out that you can really start cleaning. And waste is like dust. It is always settling in. There are many forms of waste. Lean targets them all. Anything that doesn't add value to the customer is waste.

2. The seven Lean wastes

The seven wastes were first classified by one of the pioneers of Lean thinking, Taiichi Ohno, in his classic book: *The Toyota Production System*. (Ohno, T. 1988)[3]. They are sometimes referred to as TIMWOOD to help recall.

1. Transport. Stock parts moving between activities. Physical documents moving between departments. Standard deliveries to customers. Expedited deliveries because the first delivery was wrong.

2. Inventory. Work-in-progress and stock that burns up working capital, takes up space and deteriorates over time. Emails in your inbox waiting for decisions.

3. Motion. Walking to the printer ten times a day. Searching for information. Switching between computer screens. Bending down to pick up heavy goods off the floor.

4. Waiting. Unnecessary delays, shortages of parts, requests waiting for approval. Hanging on the telephone hearing how important your call is.

5. Over-production. Producing more than the customers need.

6. Over-processing. Gold-plated solutions with features the customer doesn't want.

7. Defects. Faulty goods, application forms missing key information. Defects trigger rework. Rework triggers more rework. We've become so used to rework that it's the norm. We don't even notice it anymore. When we do something right first time, it's a pleasant surprise.

3. Other Wastes

People often focus on the above seven wastes when talking about Lean. I like to take a wider view. In fact, Taiichi Ohno stresses over and over in *The Toyota Production System* that focusing on classifications and tools and methods is not the point. It's the way of thinking that counts. In his car manufacturing environment, his categorisation was exceptionally useful and probably covered all the main forms of waste. In today's working environment, there are many other forms of waste. Here are seven of my personal favourites.

1. Distrust. Number one on my list by a long way! Distrust generates massive amounts of waste. People spending most of their time and effort covering their backs and posteriors. Producing reams of reports simply to protect their position and point the finger of blame elsewhere.

You may have heard the saying: 'You can't be creative when you're being defensive.' Most achievements require a team effort. Teams work best when they trust each other. People work best when they help each other. Most outputs are interdependent. My problems are likely caused by other factors apart from my own work. W. Edwards Deming famously summed this up in his landmark book *Out of the Crisis: 'The system is responsible for 94% of problems.'* (Deming, W. E. 1986)[4]

2. Blame culture. Let's face it, things don't go exactly to plan a lot of the time. That's reality. A functional response is, 'OK, let's figure out where we are, reflect on what we have learned, learn from it, adapt our plan accordingly and move on.' A more typical and highly wasteful response is, 'Who's to blame?' Find a scapegoat – often the wrong person – penalise or fire them and then move on. This generates waste upon waste. Creative people don't stick their necks out or take risks. Teflon-coated politicians float to the top. More energy goes into surviving than creating value. As the saying goes: 'What would you do if you weren't afraid?'

3. Leadership waste. The elephant in the room! The reality is that a lot of waste can be caused by the leadership community itself. Lack of strategic focus. Reactive crisis management. Over-engineered governance. Continually changing priorities. Too many approvals. Inability to delegate. Unclear expectations. These all cause or trigger enormous waste for those doing the work. There is an amplifier effect. A change of priority by a leader made in minutes may trigger days and weeks of wasted time and effort for their teams. Yet it is often invisible to the leadership community. They are unaware of the wasted time and effort they cause. And it's usually ignored or completely missed as an improvement target. Too dangerous. Too political. Don't go there. The only people who can fix it are the leadership community themselves. The good news is that once they decide, as a community, to remove this waste the results can be awesome. And, in my experience, once they are aware of it, they almost always decide to target and remove it. A practical way to achieve this is covered in section: **AAA Checklist Question One: Is leadership engaged and participating?**

4. Under-utilisation of skills. Highly skilled people, normally in scarce resource, wasting their time on low or no value work. Wading through approval after approval – often from people with a fraction of their expertise. Filling in unnecessary forms. Doctors, engineers, scientists, teachers, police officers, designers – experts in every field – spending valuable time on fighting the system. Chasing targets that look good upstairs but do nothing for customers. It all represents a huge waste of their skills and expertise.

5. Lack of accountability. The waste in lack of accountability is self-evident. But it's so obvious that it's often ignored.

An oil company was reviewing the disappointing results of its process improvement programme. I was asked to join the working session. One of the attendees said: 'You know our biggest single problem?' We waited to hear some super-sophisticated answer. 'Our biggest problem is people don't do what they say they are going to do. And there's no consequence. Our culture supports that behaviour. If we could fix that, this initiative would race ahead.'

6. Narcissistic behaviour. *An independent TV production company had one of the best creative departments in the industry. An expert team of about twenty people. High trust. Great teamwork. One for all and all for one. This team had created many bestselling TV shows and global franchises. These shows generated millions in revenue and had powered the rapid growth of the organisation.*

The Board recruited Tom to co-lead the department and build on the success by bringing a fresh perspective. Tom was highly political, insecure and had one agenda: Tom. His way to securing his own position was to undermine the old team and bring in his own people.

Within a few months, a superb team forged over years had imploded. By the time the CEO realised what was going on it was too late. Tom was let go but the damage was done and the team had evaporated. Years later it is still a shadow of its former self. The point is not Tom. There will always be Toms. The point is to be constantly alert to this particularly toxic and destructive form of waste.

7. Wishful thinking. How come so many projects seem on track up to the last minute? Then suddenly the bad news floods in and it turns out to be months late, way over budget and nowhere near the target specification. What could have been easily fixed when the leak was a slow trickle is now an out-of-control flood.

To recap, 3D is a framework, based on a holistic view of Lean, for flowing more value to our customers for less resource through the elimination of waste in three dimensions. Through our teams. Through our processes. Through our daily working culture.

1 Clear, J. (2020, February 4). Entropy: Why Life Always Seems to Get More Complicated. James Clear. https://jamesclear.com/entropy

2 Lascelles, J. (2016, November). A Fractal View of Lean - or why broccoli is good for you! Leancompetency.Org. https://www.leancompetency.org/lcs-articles/fractal-view-lean/

3 Ohno, T. (1988). The Toyota Production System: Beyond Large-Scale Production. Productivity Press, Portland, Oregon

4 Deming, W. E. (1986). Out of Crisis. The MIT Press.

Part Three

THE TEAM-BY-TEAM DIMENSION

None of us is as smart as all of us

- Ken Blanchard

Team-by-Team overview

TBT embeds a better way of working culture into daily working behaviours. It moves a better way of working from a project to a habit.

It is the fastest acting dimension to roll out, delivering results within days. It is straightforward to adopt because you need only get buy-in from the people directly involved. Let's say that you run a team of six people. You can get your team together, explain the general idea and then get going. Or say that you run an HR function of one hundred people split into ten teams. You can decide to roll out TBT to your entire HR function.

1. The Five Essentials

There are five essentials to the TBT way of working that inform the TBT Five Questions Checklist. Each essential is common sense. They work together to build an engine of high performance and continuous improvement in your teams. This engine becomes the culture. It becomes the norm. There is nothing complicated or difficult in these five essentials. In fact, you may read them and think: 'This is obvious, we're doing these already!' But if you do, you will be unusual. My colleagues and I have rolled out TBT to hundreds of teams and while some teams are doing some of these essentials, we rarely experience a team that is doing all of them as a matter of course. The five essentials for each team are:

1. Know your customers. Both external and internal customers. You know what your customers want and value. You know how to measure your success in meeting these wants and providing this value.

2. Engage each day as a team. This is usually starting each day with a short meeting, fifteen minutes or less, around a visual display, virtual teamboard or whiteboard. A typical agenda is to review how the team did yesterday, plans and actions for today, and a look ahead to tomorrow.

3. Understand your demand. On whatever time frame makes best sense. This might be hourly, daily, weekly or monthly. Or any other time frames that are relevant to a particular job. The team is aware of the typical volumes and variations in its demand.

4. Know your capacity, skills and what is needed. Each team is aware of its capacity as a team and the mix of skills within the team. Once this awareness is in place, it is a natural follow-on step for the team to find simple ways to increase its capacity and to fine-tune its mix of skills to better handle the variety of demand from customers.

5. Use standard ways to solve problems. Each team uses the same standard ways of solving problems depending on the type of problem concerned. This makes it easy for two or more teams to jointly solve problems.

These five essentials are the core of TBT. They work together to build a culture and engine of continuous improvement in your work environment.

2. Tea and biscuits

A TBT initiative starts with an all-team meeting. It is deliberately relaxed and informal.

I got the name 'tea and biscuits' from a client who was the finance director for a professional resourcing services company. We were reviewing the success of a TBT initiative. He said: 'It's gone well. Ahead of expectations. The key was tea and biscuits.' For a few seconds I thought it was some clever tool or statistical analysis method that I'd never heard of. I had visions of the 'tea and biscuits curve'! He explained: 'What made all the difference was sitting down with the teams right at the start and having a really informal chat about what TBT was all about, what was in it for them, getting their ideas and input and answering their questions and concerns. I call this tea and biscuits.'

It should include an open discussion on the approach and the proposed benefits that it will bring to the team. It is important to listen to any concerns and questions and get everyone's ideas and input. This is something the team is doing itself for its own benefit. Not something that is being done to the team.

A good agenda would include running through the approach using the TBT Five Questions Checklist followed by a question-and-answer session. Good discussion topics are the high-level plan, kick-off date, anticipated benefits and any risks and issues.

The most important thing about this meeting and any follow-up meetings is the personal element. How do the team members feel about this new initiative? What are their concerns? What are their thoughts and ideas that will turn it from a 'good' to a 'brilliant' initiative?

Why Team-by-Team is important

The TBT dimension is important because it directly impacts daily working culture. Many improvement initiatives struggle because they are just a series of projects. 'The priority is to improve our customer service process'; 'We need to streamline new product development'; 'We must reduce our customer queue times.' These are good goals and initiatives. But they don't change the daily ways of working. They don't embed an engine of problem solving into the fabric of the organisation. Sooner or later there will be a couple of projects that stall or go wrong. The naysayers come out of the woodwork and pour cold water on the initiative: 'I knew this wouldn't work. I told you so!'

I've seen this pattern repeated over and over again. TBT provides the foundation for a culture of continuous improvement. It gives you the bedrock to build on. It survives failures – and there will be some. It disproves the naysayers and cynics – and there will be some. Best of all, it makes your working environment more productive, higher energy and more fun.

Building this engine of continuous improvement is not just a nice to have add-on. It's a strategic asset. And one that should be nurtured and protected. While your competitors are running around firefighting and launching project after project – because that's the only way to get anything fixed – you and your colleagues are solving problems and making things better every hour, every day, every week, every month. Not as a project but as part of the job.

Team-by-Team Five Questions Checklist

Here is the TBT Five Questions Checklist. Follow and implement this checklist to experience and realise the benefits of the TBT way of working. While it is recommended that you follow the order of the checklist, it is not strictly necessary. You can experiment and have fun. Positive change will start as soon as you get going.

1. **Who are our customers and what do they want?**

2. **How do we engage each day as a team?**

3. **What does our demand look like?**

4. **What is our capacity and what skills do we need?**

5. **What are our standard ways to solve problems?**

Each of these checklist questions is explored in detail in the following sections.

1. Who are our customers and what do they want?

Plus two follow-up questions: **How do we prioritise them and how do we measure our performance?**

This question provides the essential foundation for improvement. A team exists for one purpose only and that is to add value to its customers. So this question is the foundation for the other four checklist questions.

1. Who are our customers?

Most teams will have more than one type of customer. Three, four or five customer types is quite normal. These customers can be external or internal.

For example, a customer support team in an appliance installations and repair company decides that it has four types of customer: two external and two internal. The two external types are commercial and retail customers. The two internal types are sales and field engineering.

Each customer type has their own requirements from the support team. Commercial customers want a named support person who knows their business and who they can contact direct. Retail customers want a same-day product repair or replacement. Sales need support to give a brilliant service so that customers buy again and recommend the company to their network. Field engineering need immediate and accurate data entry of all customer issues so that they can meet their 'same day repair/replacement' target.

2. What do they want?

The important thing is to focus on the fundamental purpose of the customer(s) in using the service or product that the team provides. It can be helpful to differentiate between what is sometimes called the 'voice of the customer' and the underlying purpose. They may be the same thing but sometimes they are not. Our customers may be giving us super positive feedback on how well we are fixing something that they don't want!

It was autumn, the weather was turning colder, and the billing team at a local power company was experiencing a sharp increase in calls from customers paying by direct debit. The problem was that the direct debit amounts were not large enough to cover the increased energy usage. The customers were getting into debt and receiving automatic debt notices from the company. Customers found this distressing and were calling in to complain. Why was this happening? It hadn't happened in previous years.

We did a rapid analysis. It turned out that the company had refunded any positive balances above twenty-five euros in the summer. This meant that for many customers there was too little in the tank when the weather turned colder.

The team was doing a brilliant job at adjusting the direct debit amounts and on occasion agreeing a one-off payment to sort the problem. The team was proud of its positive 'voice of customer' feedback. Responsive and friendly were typical comments.

The problem was that the team was not meeting customer purpose. The customer purpose was not to get into debt in the first place by keeping a small positive balance at all times. Not to receive negative correspondence. Not to waste time sorting it out. It was a rapid fix. A marginal increase in the direct debit refund thresholds removed ninety per cent of the calls. This was a case where it was necessary to look beneath the superficial voice of customer to address and improve the real customer purpose.

There are several ways to find out what your customers want. What is their purpose in using your product or service?

Watch them. Look at what your customers are actually doing. Explore how they are using your product and service. Analyse the types of demand that are coming in.

I was staying at a hotel on the Isle of Skye. My wife and I decided to go for a walk. It was spectacular and beautiful countryside but quite remote and rugged. Definitely a good idea to have a map. We asked at reception. 'Oh, we don't have any maps for guests,' replied the man. 'We just have the hotel one. But I'll tell you what I'll do. I'll quickly make a photocopy of a couple of pages of our map and that should sort you out.' He disappeared for a few minutes into the office behind him. He was very helpful but quite flustered as a queue of other guests was building up behind us. 'Thanks very much,' I replied. As we walked out the front door I heard another guest make the same request and get exactly the same response.

What a great opportunity to make up some interesting maps and give them to guests when they check in. Everyone wins. I'm a happy and impressed guest. The walk is more interesting. Other guests get faster service. And the receptionist is less stressed and able to do a better job.

Here is another case study that resulted in exponential sales growth from watching what customers were doing. *About 10 years ago, a rural farmer dialed into Haier's call center complaining that his washing machine was full of dirt and not functioning properly. When the technician visited the customer's home he discovered the dirt was not from the clothes the farmer wore in the field to harvest his potatoes, but rather from the harvest itself.*

41

The man had been using his washing machine to wash both clothes and potatoes. Instead of educating the farmer on how to properly use a washing machine, the technician returned to headquarters with the man's feedback. Haier subsequently released a washing machine capable of washing both clothes and potatoes, the 2009 upgraded version of which led Haier to become the number one provider of laundry equipment in the entire world. (Backaler, J. 2010)[1] What a great example of finding out what customers want by observing and reacting.

Ask them. Probably the most obvious way is to ask them. You might imagine that teams always do this anyway. You would be surprised. The first exercise on the 3D TBT course is for each team to ask its customers what they want. The most common reaction is: 'Good idea, we haven't done that for ages!' It doesn't need to be over-engineered. Keep it simple. Ask open-ended questions so that the customer has the headroom to really explain what they value. Once the customer gets talking, don't interrupt. It often takes people a bit of time to get to what they really want and value. Resist the temptation to ask a follow-up question just as the customer is saying: 'So what I really want is…' Once interrupted, they may never get back to it. Just listen and take notes.

How many customers to ask? Be pragmatic and flexible. One approach is to start with five customers of each type. If they all say exactly the same thing then that is probably sufficient. If they all say something different then ask another five customers and so on until clusters emerge. Here are some good open-ended questions to get started: 'What is your purpose in using our product/service?'; 'What is important to you in using our product/service?'; 'What do you really need from our product/service?'

Anticipate them. There are many examples of winning customers by anticipating what they want or meeting the underlying purpose that the customers themselves were unaware of. Steve Jobs put it like this: '*Some people say give the customers what they want. But that's not my approach. Our job is to figure out what they're going to want before they do. I think Henry Ford once said, "If I'd asked customers what they wanted, they would have told me, 'A faster horse!'" People don't know what they want until you show it to them. That's why I never rely on market research. Our task is to read things that are not yet on the page.*' (Aten, J. 2021, January)[2]

3. How do we prioritise them?

This is the third part of the question and it's often missed. The reality is that it's not possible to keep everyone happy all the time. Choices have to be made. This question generates a valuable discussion on which type(s) of customer we need to focus on delighting. And which can take second or third place if necessary. It uncovers situations where teams have been totally focusing on one type of customer at the expense of others.

The legal team of a consumer products company consisted of eight highly qualified lawyers. They saw their job - first and foremost - as protecting the organisation from legal issues. The colleagues who used their services came a long way second. And it showed. They did not have a good reputation with the business. They were seen as slow, unresponsive and arrogant. The perception from the business was that when a contract went to legal for drafting or review, it went into a black hole. And when you enquired what was happening, the answers were terse and abrupt!

Marie, the head of the legal team, was really enthused with the concept of multiple customer types and prioritising them. 'I guess that we've always prioritised the organisation as our number one customer and everyone else a distant third. Maybe we should look at this again.' She and her team met with colleagues from around the business and asked them what they wanted. The answers had similar themes. Responsive, transparent and predictable service. Plus courtesy. Lose the arrogance. We're all in this together.

Marie met with her team. They quickly came up with a set of changes that met these requirements without jeopardising their primary responsibility to the organisation. Marie reflected, 'The organisation is still our number one priority. That's how it should be. But our internal colleagues are now a much higher number two. We'd lost sight of that somehow and this exercise helped us rectify this.'

4. How do we measure our performance?

Once we know who our customers are, what they want and how to prioritise them, the next step is to assess how well we are doing. The key is to use measures linked to what our customers want. Again, asking the customer is a good place to start. Use open-ended questions such as: 'How do you judge how well we are doing in meeting your requirements?'; 'What criteria are important to you?'

It is essential to use measures that reflect the customers' purpose in using the team. Two reasons. First, because these are the measures that will truly reflect how well the team is doing. Second, and just as important, because using the wrong measures may well drive the wrong behaviours in the team. Behaviours that may be opposite to what the customer values and wants. What you measure is what you get and if you are measuring the wrong thing, you will get the wrong thing.

A retail company wanted to improve the performance of the debt collection teams. I spent an afternoon listening to the advisors on the phones calling customers who were in arrears. I sat with one advisor and listened to a couple of calls that were impressively handled. On the third though, I noticed that he wasn't quite as persuasive as on the previous ones, even though the customer seemed a lot more likely and willing to pay their bill. At the end of the call I asked him why that was. 'That's simple,' he replied. 'I could have easily got that customer to pay. However, their current bill becomes debt in two days' time. I'll set a reminder for then and call them back and get them to pay then, that way my stats will be better.' It turned out that the advisor's performance measurement was based almost solely on the financial value of debt he collected. By waiting for a few days for the customer to accrue more debt, he was able to collect £600 rather than £350. The team was allowing customers to go into debt so that the collections 'performance' looked better! Measures were driving behaviours that no one wanted.

The solution was fast, simple and zero cost. New measures were introduced that aligned with customer purpose and focused on the number of accounts cleared rather than the cash collected per month. This better served the customer. It also resulted in the average time to collect reducing from sixty to eighteen days and the value collected per person per day increasing by ninety-four per cent.

Discarding flawed measures and using measures aligned to customer purpose is a super quick win. It costs nothing, has immediate impact, better serves the customer and makes the job more fulfilling for the team.

2. How do we engage each day as a team?

This question has a rapid and highly visible impact on the team's culture and daily ways of working. Many teams do not really engage on a daily basis as a team. People come in, sit down, pick up where they left off the day before, head down and get on with it. That's the norm. That's what we've always done.

David had a problem yesterday completing his work. He has had a sleepless night and is stressed about today. He decides not to tell Anna, his boss. He doesn't want to look weak and out of control. His colleagues are completely unaware that he's struggling. If they were, they would intervene to help. The next day he's even further behind, makes a serious mistake and it causes a major issue.

This question **'How do we engage each day as a team?'** changes this dynamic.

1. The daily huddle

The team starts each day with a short meeting around a physical or virtual whiteboard that the team has designed specifically for this purpose. The meeting is ten to fifteen minutes long. It is often called a team huddle and the whiteboard is called a huddle board. **Please see an illustration of a virtual huddle in Figure 3.1**. Team members from different locations are all looking at the same whiteboard on their screens and communicating in real-time.

The meeting has a tight agenda. It covers the following items, usually in this order:

How each team member is feeling today. Often done using tick marks next to smiley faces going from happy to average to sad. This can relate just to work or include outside work as well. It is the team's choice and each team member's choice. No right or wrong. One minute.

Review the previous day. Team's performance against agreed measures? Backlogs? Issues and problems? Opportunities? Can be just the previous day or week to date. Whatever works best. What went wrong? Plan to fix it? Five minutes.

Plan for today. Expected demand? Team capacity? Who is doing what? Work scheduling? Priorities for the day? Planned and unplanned absence? Who is overcapacity and needs help? Who is undercapacity and can offer help? Five minutes.

Looking ahead. Coaching and training plans? Team up-skilling and cross-skilling? Joiners, movers, leavers? Summary of in-flight improvements? Escalations required? Three minutes.

Celebrating success. Finish on a positive note. Celebrate what's gone well. Who has just done a brilliant job? Highlighted an issue? Developed a new skill? One minute.

A key feature of the morning huddle is that every item is relevant to the present. The meeting gets the team geared up and thinking as a team for the coming day. Problems are made visible. Priorities and issues are agreed and reinforced. Interventions are planned. **Please see an illustration of a huddle board in Figure 3.2.** Notice that today's performance gets centre stage and is updated throughout the day. The time is 2pm. Can you see which activity is behind schedule and how the team plan to rectify this?

Figure 3.1 Huddle team in action

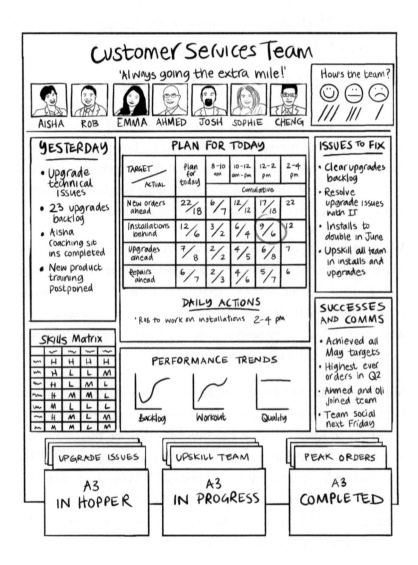

Figure 3.2 Huddle board example

2. Impact of the daily huddle

The daily huddle has a profound impact on a team's psyche and behaviours. Much bigger than might at first be apparent. What are these impacts and why are they so psychologically powerful?

We care about each other. This is the first message that the huddle conveys. It is how the huddle starts. How am I and how are you today? We are not robots. Everyone has a mass of stuff going on under the surface. Work pressures, home pressures, finances, relationships, health, kids, schools, parents. It is great just to take a few minutes out at the start of the day and acknowledge our humanity and be aware of each other as human beings and as a team.

We are across it. We are professional. We know what our customers want. We know how to measure our performance. We understand our demand. We know our capacity and the skills we need. Of course there will be issues. There always are. But we don't just live with them. We continuously improve. We welcome problems. How can we improve if there are no problems?

Shines a light. The huddle makes things visible. And the huddle board plays a key role in this visibility. And making something visible is halfway to fixing it. What was our performance yesterday? What is the target and plan today and how are we doing against it? Who is over and undercapacity? Who is stressed? Who is struggling? Who has got some spare capacity to help others? What are the team's pinch points? Where are we letting our customers down? Where could we do better? What is coming down the road?

A physical huddle board should be situated where everyone can see it during the day, not just at the morning huddle itself. Virtual huddle boards should be on a shared folder. It is normally updated by the team members during the day. It is a living, breathing thing. It changes through the day. And the huddle board communicates to others outside the team. When colleagues and visitors drop in, they can look at the huddle board and see who is in the team, what the team does, how it measures itself and how it is doing. What is the reaction? Wow! This is the A team. These guys are on top of their game.

Call to action. Actions for today. Actions for tomorrow. Coaching actions. Improvement actions. Problem-solving actions. Training actions. Escalation actions. The morning huddle and the huddle board are the centre of this call to action. It's where it all comes together. It's the drumbeat.

Impacts me. The huddle impacts each team member as an individual. It increases pride and a feeling of belonging. In being part of the team. Everyone prefers to be part of a winning team and the huddle helps teams win. Everyone prefers to have delighted happy customers, external or internal. The huddle puts the customer front of mind every day. Not once a quarter. Not at a customer first seminar. Not at a training course. But every day. In the front line. In my team. That's what we do. That's why we're here.

This is ours. The best huddle agendas and visuals are designed by the teams themselves. The team owns them because they developed them and believe in them. This story from a production manager lands the point.

A production manager at an aircraft engine manufacturer created what he thought was an excellent piece of visual management. A huddle board that improved the planning process, made decision making out of office hours easier and highlighted missed maintenance tasks. From his perspective it was a big success. A work of art. But the team didn't like it. One of the team approached him to share their feelings and how they wanted to change it. His ego was bruised but he agreed to the changes. The important thing was that the team now owned it. It was theirs. They made sure that it worked well. In fact, they never stopped tweaking and improving it.

3. Developing new skills

Facilitating the morning huddle is a useful development skill. It can be challenging. You need to keep it moving. Achieve the fifteen-minute deadline. Park longer discussions for off-line follow-up. Keep people engaged. Make it fun. Once the team leader has got the huddle up and running, they can ask team members to take turns in leading it. It's a good coaching opportunity. 'Lucy, this is your week to lead the huddle. How can you make it a bit crisper this time?' 'Ben, I observed the team's attention wandered yesterday. How can you keep everyone fully engaged?'

The huddle creates a belief that we care about each other, problems will get fixed, root causes will get figured out, pinch points will get sorted, issues resolved. It's not problems that get people down and depressed. It's the feeling that they'll never get fixed. The huddle blows that away. It is a blast of oxygen into the team. As the saying goes: 'See together, know together, act together!'

4. A cascade of huddles

The huddle system should cascade upwards so that problems raised by the teams get rapidly escalated to the colleagues with the authority and resources to fix them. A typical scenario is that the team leaders have their own huddle immediately following their team huddles. This means that any problems raised by the teams are immediately discussed by the people who can do something about it.

Here is a simple example.

Mahmoud is a member of the service team. He raises the issue that they are receiving an increasing number of late transaction updates from the sales team. They need these updates by three in the afternoon to get them processed. But in the last two days over twenty-five per cent of the transactions have been received after the deadline. The service team is getting criticism from field engineering for late updates which mess up their next day schedules. Mahmoud raises this with Sara who is his service team leader. Sara immediately raises it at the team leader huddle with Adrian who leads the sales team. Adrian promises to look into it and update her the next day. It turns out that a new recruit to the sales team was unaware of the three o'clock deadline. The problem is resolved.

The cascade of huddles can go up two or three or four levels. Whatever is needed to get rapid awareness and decision making.

Combined Cycle Gas Turbines (CCGT) are a form of electricity generation technology that combines a gas-fired turbine with a steam turbine.

We were working with the manager of a plant that had three CCGT units. Each housed in a building the size of a football pitch and as tall as a cathedral. There were around sixty highly skilled people on-site and twelve teams split between four departments: Engineering; Services; Operations; and Maintenance. The plant operated twenty-four hours, seven days a week with three shifts. The plant manager was a passionate believer and leader in Lean ways of working. He had organised a cascade of huddles that ensured that decision makers at every level were immediately aware of current performance information and any issues. There was a huddle for each shift change. Each team had a daily huddle at 8 am. The team leaders had their daily huddle at 8.30 am. The plant manager and his leadership team had their daily huddle at 9 am. Issues and decisions required from the team huddles were immediately acted on. It was a well-oiled communication, decision-making and action machine as you might expect in this high-intensity environment; all based on a carefully orchestrated cascade of huddles.

3. What does our demand look like?

This question has an immediate impact on the team in terms of the insights and improvement ideas that it generates. You might think that every team would know the demand volumes and variations that it is dealing with. You'd be surprised. Teams often don't. They have become so used to just coping and firefighting that this basic analysis gets overlooked.

Why is it so essential that a team should understand its demand? Because it is the primary driver behind the size of the team and the mix of skills that is needed to handle its customers' requirements. It informs how work should be allocated. Who should do what and in what order. It highlights whether the team is in control or not. Are invisible backlogs building up that will cause major disruption in hours, days or weeks? Without a clear understanding of its demand, a team is flying blind. This can be the underlying cause of many problems and issues that the team is facing. Getting a clear understanding of demand can point the way to solutions and innovations that the team may never have considered; many of them quick and simple to implement.

1. Capturing team demand

The good news is that analysing team demand is straightforward. It is all within the remit and scope of the team. The team just has to look at itself. The team looks at itself in three ways. Looking backwards. Looking at today. Looking forwards. Nominate two or three members of the team to look at each view. Involving six to nine colleagues in the demand analysis drives engagement and hands-on participation. Give each group its own physical or virtual whiteboard to start building a visual demand picture. Use Post-it notes and Sharpie pens because it makes it easy to keep modifying and improving. Leave a space to write the main messages, insights and next steps.

Looking backwards. The 'looking backwards' team collates all existing available information on past demand. Daily, weekly, monthly and annual totals are a good starting point. This always generates useful insights and learnings. 'We never realised that thirty per cent of our monthly demand comes in the last week of the month. No wonder the team is so stressed each month end!' It also highlights gaps. 'It would be really useful to understand demand patterns through the day on an hourly basis but we just don't have this information. I'll ask the 'looking at today' team to start collecting this.'

Looking at today. This team designs and updates a daily demand board throughout the day. This is often the centre section of the team's huddle board. The team is capturing what is actually happening at a new level of granularity. 'We'd never noticed the late afternoon demand surge each Tuesday and Thursday. Let's find out why that's happening.' Use whatever time interval makes most sense. Hourly is always a good starting point.

Looking forward. This team explores ways to improve the accuracy of demand forecasting going forward. The more accurate the forecast, the better the team is able to adjust its capability and skill set to handling the demand. This is where the three viewpoints support each other. Looking backwards provides the data for the looking forward team to analyse for patterns and trends previously overlooked. Understanding today's demand in greater detail may provide clues as to what will happen tomorrow.

2. Analysing team demand

The process of capturing demand normally takes a few days. This is a great learning exercise. As a result, the team will have started to understand and anticipate its demand to new levels of accuracy and insight. The foundation is now in place for more detailed analysis. Here are five of the most insightful ways to analyse your team's demand and unlock potential opportunities. Consider which ways might be helpful for your team.

Value vs failure demand. This is such a powerful concept that it deserves to go first. It can simultaneously improve customer service and free up a team's capacity. Value demand is handling any type of demand that is providing value to the customer. A customer calling into a customer support team to report a lost credit card is value demand. The team is providing clear value to the customer in dealing with this situation. A customer calling in to ask why her statement has not arrived is failure demand. This demand is only happening because of a failure somewhere in the system. The golden rule is simple: remove failure demand and improve handling value demand.

A wealth management company had over sixty-five different forms covering its range of products, services and customer interactions. They were available on-line but were basically digital copies of the original paper forms with minimal error checking. Many forms asked for more information than was actually needed. Eight of the forms accounted for ninety-five per cent of the volume. Around six thousand of these eight forms were completed each year. The paper forms had been developed by different people within the organisation over several years. With little or no testing for user friendliness or error proofing.

During our analysis phase we discovered that less than sixty per cent of the forms were completed correctly. Forty-two per cent had errors of one sort or another. Missing information. Mistyped email addresses. Incomplete telephone numbers. Wrong form. To be fair, it was difficult not to make a mistake.

This caused a continual wave of failure demand and rework for both the company and their clients. Their clients were brokers or third-party intermediaries. Busy people under pressure who did not appreciate their time being wasted. It also caused a continual stream of bad data to go into the organisation's systems and databases. This situation had continued for years. We estimated the failure demand at over fifty per cent because of the knock-on errors and rework.

As part of our improvements, we redesigned and renamed the existing forms using proven form design principles combined with extensive user testing. This reduced incorrect forms from forty-two to nineteen per cent. Not perfect, but a move in the right direction. Rule one: remove failure demand. The redesigned forms asked for less information in an easier flow and took about half the time to complete. Altogether a better customer experience. Rule two: improve handling value demand.

Customer type. The team needs to understand the volumes of demand by type of customer. Most teams have more than one type of customer.

An operations team is simultaneously dealing with sales, service, credit and engineering. They only have one person with the skills to handle engineering. This leads to constant delays handling engineering requests. These delays in turn trigger knock-on problems for the end customers – and from there for sales and service.

Going down a level, the team needs to understand the volumes of demand for each type of product and service. Does the team have the right mix of skills to handle the demand? Then look at the volumes of each type of product and service over whatever time frames are most helpful to measure. This might be hourly, daily, weekly, monthly or annually. Pay special attention to the peaks and troughs and the team capacity pinch points. Different customers often need to be worked differently. The team needs standard ways to handle the variation.

Priority. The prioritisation rules that govern how demand is handled can provide the key to fixing problems.

The service team of a leading European pension provider handled a large number of different types of customer interactions. One particularly difficult interaction was when the customer changed job and wanted to have their pension transferred. Customer complaints were frequent and heated.

I worked with two colleagues from the service team to explore and fix the problem. We found that lead times were between two to six months for about five to ten hours of actual work! Truly astonishing. As part of the demand analysis, we categorised demand by priority into four levels. Then we tracked what happened to the work in each priority level.

The key lay in how customer service colleagues were incentivised to prioritise their work. New business enquiries were priority one. Agents received financial rewards for increasing revenues. Urgent enquiries were priority two. This avoided escalations and complaints. Easy enquiries were priority three. Change of address for example. These helped agents to make their daily quotas. Pension transfers were priority four. Guess what? Agents hardly ever got round to priority four. Priority fours would go straight to the bottom of the pile and stay there. For months at a time. Changing the prioritisation rules and incentives was the key to fixing the problem. It slashed the lead times and, best of all, it was free. In fact, it saved money because the new business rewards were scrapped. They encouraged the wrong behaviour. They did more harm than good. The prioritisation lens had enabled a rapid low-cost solution.

Outcome. Another interesting way to look at demand is by outcome.

The mortgage underwriting team of an African bank analysed the outcomes of their underwriting decisions over the previous year. There were just over four thousand five hundred mortgage applications per year. Their analysis showed that they had declined around one thousand seven hundred of these applications. The CEO took one look at their analysis and said, 'What do we offer these people instead? Surely we must be able to offer some of them a more appropriate product or a smaller home loan?' 'No,' was the reply. 'We don't offer them anything. In fact, we don't even stay in touch.' It was a call to action. A suite of alternative offers was developed together with training for the team. Over a quarter of declined applicants ended up taking an alternative product and becoming new customers.

Process and geography. Teams usually have multiple processes flowing through them. For example, a customer service team is simultaneously dealing with orders, exchanges, fulfilment, customer queries and complaints. The team needs to be constantly evaluating its capacity and skill set to handle the variation. Countries have widely different rules and regulations. This can cause an exponential increase in demand variation.

A UK-based software company had a small expert HR team of ten people. They were highly experienced and comfortably coped with the UK HR processes. The company was growing at over twenty per cent a year, much of it driven by growing demand from outside the UK. This included North America, Germany, Singapore and Brazil. People started working in these new locations. The UK HR team was suddenly dealing with four different variations of their six core processes. That's twenty-four process variations! Complexity increased exponentially. Inevitably mistakes started to be made. The necessary knowledge and experience just wasn't there. The team was swamped and stressed. The blame game started. Key people resigned making the situation even worse. It took a special project over a year to get the situation rectified and back on an even keel.

In this section we looked at **TBT Checklist Question Three: What does our demand look like?** The case studies show what a powerful question this is. Not only for signposting the way to excellent performance but for resolving problems and revealing exciting opportunities to innovate and improve.

4. What is our capacity and what skills do we need?

This question has two objectives. First, help the team focus its time on value-add work and remove the activities that are not adding value. Second, help the team build the right mix of skills to handle the work coming in.

Focusing capacity on value-add work

Although we may come to work eight hours a day, we don't actually have eight hours to spend on value-adding activities. We have less time. Lunch breaks, coffee breaks, meetings, non-essential emails, random telephone calls: our time can quickly get eaten up. People are often stressed and overcapacity. 'We don't have enough people.' 'There's never enough time in the day.' 'My work-life balance is shot to pieces!' These are frequently heard comments. 3D uses two tools to free up capacity and enable more enjoyable working with better outcomes: The Apple Tree and MyDay.

1. The Apple Tree

The Apple Tree gives you a simple and collaborative way to quickly free up capacity. It's all about low hanging fruit. Imagine that you and a friend are hungry, standing by an apple tree and longing for a delicious juicy crunchy apple. There are a couple of perfect apples four feet off the ground, another three at seven feet and another two at ten feet. Which apples are you going to pick? Easy, right? The two apples at four feet. The low hanging fruit.

It's the same with freeing up capacity. The Apple Tree diagram has branches at four feet, seven feet and ten feet. It comes with eight recommended 'ways' (eight apples) to free up capacity. So that you can focus on customer value work, reduce team stress and increase performance. The Apple Tree exercise is not about letting people go. It's about letting customer dissatisfaction, stress and waste go! Here are the eight types of apple. They are just a starter. You can probably think of others. Great, go for it!

1. Remove failure demand. Probably the single quickest and highest impact way to free up capacity for value-add work. And it's a double whammy because it gives the customer a better outcome at the same time.

A water provider was rolling out TBT way of working. One team focused on meter reads submitted by customers that contained errors. They generated a new bill even if a bill had just gone out. On review of this it became apparent that a large proportion of these errors had a marginal impact to the bill and would automatically rectify the following month through standard processing. Adjustments to the acceptance criteria in the system reduced this failure demand by seventy-five per cent. The outcome? Less customer disruption through a second and unnecessary bill. Three of the four colleagues were able to move on to more interesting and value-add work. And a follow-up initiative was launched to make it easier for customers to read their own meter and get it right first time.

2. Reduce meetings. Meetings grow like weeds. Treat them as such! Prune them on a regular basis by asking a series of basic questions that can quickly free up capacity: 'Do we need this meeting at all? Can we reduce the duration; the frequency; the attendees?' This is also a good opportunity to increase the effectiveness of meetings. To turn the time from low to high value-add. Some good questions to ask: 'What's the purpose of this meeting? What type of meeting is this? Information sharing? Decision-making? Other? Do we have the right agenda and attendees? Could we combine this meeting into another meeting?'

3. Use the current best way. There is almost always a best way to do something. Or at least a current best way because there's always room for improvement. There's usually someone in the team who knows how to do it. Or actually does it! Their knowledge can save hours, days and weeks of time for the rest of the team. But it often remains a secret. Maybe they are a bit embarrassed and don't want to seem a show-off. Or don't realise that they are much faster and more effective than their colleagues. Or no one has thought to share the best way.

I was coaching the CEO of a highly successful recruitment company. He was an amazing source of 'best way' knowledge. From years of experience he knew the best way to talk to clients, to qualify prospects in or out, to organise his work, when to chase and when to leave alone, how to achieve his revenue goals. His team worked in one big room. He could observe and hear his colleagues all day. And it drove him nuts! He heard and watched them doing things in a 'not-best way' over and over again. But he said nothing. It wasn't his style. My coaching boiled down to 'David, you owe it to your colleagues to pass on your knowledge and train them in all these best ways. Make it part of their expectations from day one that you will do this. Make it part of the initial interview. That way it won't be intrusive or threatening. It will just be the culture.' He was a great learner and immediately pivoted to this new approach. It had instant results. His colleagues appreciated his new helpful constructive coaching style. They achieved more. He felt better. This simple change of sharing best ways had a fundamental impact on the success and growth of his company.

4. Move work to the right place. Sometimes work ends up being done by the wrong team. Usually by accident or force of habit.

Moving it to the right team is an instant capacity win. And the customers will likely get a better service.

The back-office operations team for a large retailer was analysing its activities as preparation for an Apple Tree session. They were continually stressed, had large backlogs which meant unhappy customers and often worked until 8 pm or later. It turned out that thirty-five per cent of their activities were actually the responsibility of other teams! They were expert and naturally helpful people and had become the go-to source of knowledge for questions that had nothing to do with their core work. It was an easy fix. Each team member was given an up-to-date referral list of where to pass these activities. Within two weeks the incidental work emails and calls had dried up. The additional capacity cleared the backlogs and gave them the headroom to provide better customer service. Late working became the exception rather than the norm.

5. Look for hidden capacity leakages. It can sometimes be confusing why theoretical performance on paper isn't translated into the real world. One good question to ask: 'Are we looking at the full job?'

A team of machinists working on submarine power plants – complex nuclear-powered engines roughly the size of thirteen lorries – were struggling to understand why their machining steps were taking longer than expected. It was because the time to alter the set-up of the machine required specialist lifting skills from the crane operators that often involved a wait. While the time to complete the machining was known, and the machine never left the machining area, these specialist cranage skills were a hidden bottleneck in the process and understanding this was key to getting the work to move on more quickly.

6. Improve processes. This is often the instinctive starting point for people when they are considering how to free up capacity. 'We need to improve our processes' is a common refrain. And they are right. The paradox though is that it's often not the low hanging fruit. It can be the apple at seven or ten feet. You may need a step ladder to get to it. It can take a fair amount of time and effort to make it happen. Improving processes is a must-do action for freeing up capacity. But it's not always the first must-do action. There may be much lower hanging fruit on the apple tree.

7. Target and remove all types of waste. The seventh apple is a catch all. Waste consumes time. Waste consumes precious capacity. The team should review the section: **Grounded in Lean thinking** for a list of the types of waste to target and remove.

8. Re-balance skills to demand. This is such a large and delicious apple that it has its own section: **Building the right skills**.

How do you run an Apple Tree session with your teammates? Here are the steps:

1. Write the names of the above eight types of apple on their own Post-it note. You may think of additional types of apple. Great, write these on their own Post-it as well.

2. Decide on the size of opportunity of each apple and draw an apple of a specific size on each Post-it note to reflect this. The bigger the opportunity the bigger the apple.

3. Discuss as a team where to place each apple on the tree. At four or seven or ten feet. Then place each apple on the tree at its appropriate height.

4. Agree which apples to pick in which order.

The reason The Apple Tree exercise works well is because it is a simple, quick and fun way to have the right discussions on what can be a sensitive subject. **Please see an illustration of an Apple Tree in Figure 3.3**. Notice how the team have selected the lowest

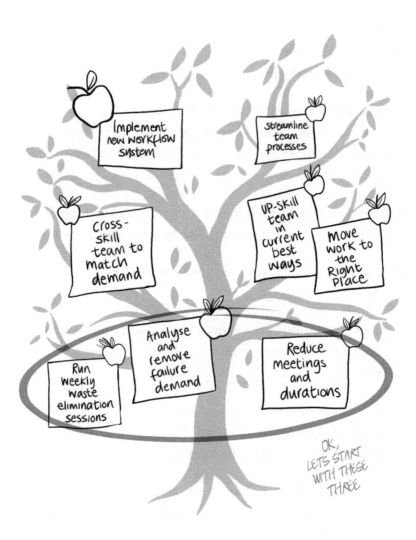

Figure 3.3 Apple Tree example

hanging fruit over the biggest opportunities. You can download a blank Apple Tree template from **the3dworkplace.com**.

2. MyDay

This is a simple tool to help team members track how they are spending their time. The principle of being 'approximately right rather than precisely wrong' is fine. Colleagues don't need to know to the nearest minute exactly what they are doing. They just need enough insight to spot and address the obvious opportunity areas.

There are many different variations depending on the type of work involved. The success of a MyDay analysis depends on two things: a helpful categorisation of the work types; and running it over a sufficient duration to throw up all the issues and opportunities.

Please see an illustration of a MyDay completed by a teacher in Figure 3.4. In this example the teacher, Emma, has done more than simply capture her activities, times and perceived value-add. She has used the opportunity to think through how she could actually add more value to several of them.

There is a variation on MyDay called MyWeek. This is typically used for team leaders to track how they are spending their time. Their time commitments often have a weekly rather than a daily cadence and MyWeek is better at capturing this. A common issue is that they are not spending enough time 'in the work', seeing and experiencing what's actually happening on the ground. The MyWeek analysis is used to find the time to do this.

My Day : Emma, Class Teacher

Time	Duration	Activity	Category	Value add (1-5)
7.00 7.45	45	Driving to school	Travel	1
7.45 8.20	35	Preparing classroom and resources (SHARE PREP SLIDES WITH OTHERS)	Preparation	2 (3)
8.20 8.30	10	Coffee in staffroom & chat with colleagues	Social	2
8.30- 8.50	20	Playground duty (OBSERVE SPECIFIC CHILDREN'S SOCIAL INTERACTION)	Supervision	2 (4)
8.50- 9.00	10	Registration	Admin	2
9.00- 9.15	15	Attend whole school assembly (USE TIME TO REFLECT ON FINE TUNING LESSONS PLANNED)	Supervision	2 (4)
9.15- 10.30	75	English lesson (REFLECT AND REVISE LESSON AS I GO ALONG)	Teaching	4 (5)
10.30- 10.45	15	Playground duty (OBSERVE SPECIFIC CHILDREN)	Supervision	2 (4)
10.45 12.00	75	Maths lesson (CHANGE PACE OF LESSON TO REFLECT LEARNING NEEDS)	Teaching	4 (5)
12.00 12.40	40	Marking and preparation for an afternoon (WORK WITH SPECIFIC CHILDREN GIVING INSTANT FEEDBACK)	Preparation	2 (5)
12.40- 1.00	20	Lunch	Personal	2
1.00- 2.15	75	Humanities lesson (DECIDED TO USE CHILDRENS IDEAS IN FUTURE LESSON)	Teaching	4 (5)
2.15- 2.30	15	Tea break	Personal	2
2.30- 3.15	45	Review of learning, finishing off work and storytime	Teaching	4
3.15- 6.00	165	Marking, and catch up with year group colleagues to review and revise lesson plans	Teaching	5

Figure 3.4 MyDay example

3. Making it real

This case study shows the role that MyDay and MyWeek can play in triggering positive outcomes.

A commercial real estate agency was struggling to cope with increasing client expectations and managing the cost to serve them. One of the biggest problems was client arrears, running into tens of millions of dollars and getting bigger all the time. Collecting client arrears was an extremely time-consuming and manual job and the finance team simply didn't have the capacity to stay on top of the demand.

The team decided to use the MyDay approach to help them truly understand how they were spending their time between value and non-value activities. They were shocked and frustrated to find that only twenty-two per cent of time was actually adding value! The rest was spent on non-value activities including handling failure demand running at fifty to sixty per cent of all demand.

This was a massive wake-up call and led to a relentless focus on improving performance by analysing and removing the root causes of the failure demand. They adopted two measurements to judge their success: the size of the client arrears backlog and the percentage of time spent on value-add activities.

Over the next nine months they created an additional thirty per cent capacity within the existing team. This capacity resulted in client arrears being reduced by £10m with a parallel cost saving of sixteen per cent by not replacing leavers and cutting back on contractors. The percentage of time on value-add activities increased from twenty-two to fifty-three per cent. A positive move and a lot more to go for. The team made MyWeek a permanent fixture for each person every month in order to sustain and further improve their performance.

Building the right skills

Most teams will do a variety of work. Very few teams will be doing just one thing and therefore require only one skill set. So most teams require a combination of skills in the right amounts to handle the demand. Not too much, which means people have nothing to do. Not too little, which means queues and backlogs. In addition, there will be variation in the amounts of each type of work.

Let's use a simple example.

The average daily incoming demand into the application processing team is forty complex applications, fifty standard applications and thirty simple applications. We have a team of five people. They are all skilled to handle simple applications, four are skilled to handle standard applications and only one colleague, Pierre, is skilled to handle complex applications. What's going to happen? There's going to be a backlog of complex applications. Pierre is going to be overcapacity, over-worked and stressed out. Other team members may be sitting around with nothing to do. We have a capacity imbalance. We need to rapidly up-skill additional team members to handle complex applications.

Sometimes it's not just a case of building the right skills. It's organising those skills into the right combinations to handle the work in the most effective manner.

A department assessed whether people with medical problems, injuries or disabilities were fit and able to drive. The operations manager who led the area was hearing concerns from his team that cases were taking too long to be assessed and for final decisions to be made.

Walking out onto the floor, the size of the issue became apparent. The people working in the team were organised by level of experience.

The newest joiners sat at one end. Their role was to scan the incoming work onto the system. Next to them were a large number of Level One colleagues whose job it was to assess the cases, follow the procedures in their work instructions and send drivers for the relevant tests required to assess their fitness to drive. The test results would come back and whenever a Level One colleague lacked the knowledge or experience to know what to do, they would pass the results onto a Level Two colleague to assess and make a decision. There were also Level Three and Level Four colleagues who would handle increasingly more complex cases and finally Level Five was a group of fully qualified medical doctors who had elected to leave their practices and join the drivers medical assessment team.

The doctors would frequently complain that a complex case had taken months to reach them as it slowly wound its way up through the levels, only for the doctor to make a decision that the driver should immediately stop driving as their condition was too dangerous for them to be on the road!

The solution was obvious. The department was re-organised into multi-skilled teams with a Level Five doctor at the centre surrounded by a balanced number of Level Three/Four and Level One/Two team members. Everyone had a buddy and whenever a case came in that someone didn't know what to do with, they could ask the more senior person sitting next to them. Another change was to how the team was measured. Individual targets on the number of tasks a person could complete were scrapped. Instead, the team was measured on how quickly a final, accurate decision could be made about someone's fitness to drive.

The change was profound. Cases were decided in hours and days, not weeks and months. And the rate of up-skilling and cross-skilling rose sharply as people learnt from each other as a natural by-product of doing the work together.

The starting point is to have a clear idea of the volume and variation of work coming in. The good news is that we already know this from **TBT Checklist Question Three: What does our demand look like?** This is an example of the TBT Five Checklist Questions working together. Once we know the demand, we can work out the required amount of capability and skills. 3D uses two tools to do this. The Skills Matrix and an extension of the Skills Matrix: The Skills and Demand Matrix.

1. Skills Matrix

This tool shows both the current and target level of skills within the team. The typical format is to list the team members down the left-hand side and the types of skills across the top. Then to agree how to classify the levels of competence for each skill type. Two common formats are 'Low, Medium, High' and 'None, Learning, Competent, Expert'. The four-level format has more granularity. This can be helpful. For example, 'Expert' could signify people who can train their colleagues.

It's important to write short definitions of each skill level so everyone has the same understanding. Use whatever format works best for your team and environment.

The team leader meets with each colleague and together they agree their current level of competence for each skill. They also agree where they'd like to get to in terms of skills development. This in turn informs their personal training and development plan. Not everyone needs to be an expert in every skill. Not everyone wants to be. Using a Skills Matrix has three main benefits. It creates an awareness of the different skills required to meet customer demand and provides transparency on the skill levels in the team. It recognises the skills of individual team members and the effort they are making to further develop their skills. It drives the training and development plan for each colleague.

At the same time, the Skills Matrix has some hazards to avoid. Lucas thinks he is an expert in interviewing skills while his manager thinks he is competent. Emma is upset that she is the least skilled person in the team. James thinks that John's skill levels have been overstated. The team leader can navigate these hazards by setting a clear context up front that the Skills Matrix is purely to support the team, its success and the development ambitions of its members. **Please see an illustration of a Skills Matrix for a real estate team in Figure 3.5**. The team members have each selected their priority area for personal development ahead of the next review.

2. Skills and Demand Matrix

This is a natural extension of the Skills Matrix. The Skills and Demand Matrix uses the demand data from TBT Checklist Question Three to show the range of skills that is actually required to do the work. You can download an example Skills and Demand Matrix at **the3dworkplace.com**. Putting Skills and Demand side by side highlights any gaps between the actual skills in the team and the skills required to handle the work. It is a must-have tool for capacity planning as well as training and development. As always, it is pure common sense. Step one is to work out the skills required for each type of activity. Step two is to list the daily volumes of each activity. Step three is to multiply the skills by the volumes to give the daily capacity requirement of each skill type. Comparing this to the Skills Matrix shows where we have imbalances between the skills required by the demand coming in and the actual skills in the team.

I'VE CIRCLED OUR AGREED DEVELOPMENT PRIORITIES

Skills	Real Estate Team Members				
	Prisha	Tom	Camilla	Pedro	Sarah
Sales and negotiation	4	3	(2)	(1)	1
Administration	2	2	3	2	3
Local area knowledge	4	4	2	1	(1)
Industry rules and regulations	(3)	4	2	2	1
Personal network	4	2	2	4	1
Specialization (eg: upmarket)	3	(2)	3	1	1

Skill definitions
1. No experience
2. Limited experience and learning
3. Competent
4. Expert and coaching colleagues

Figure 3.5 Skills Matrix example

5. What are our standard ways to solve problems?

People get a great feeling of empowerment when they see a problem as a team. They combine their expertise as a team. They solve the problem and enjoy the benefits as a team. A common reaction is: 'We really can fix things around here. It's within our gift and power. We can make change happen.'

TBT Checklist Question Five is not just about tools and techniques. It's about the behaviours of solving problems. It encompasses when, where and who as much as how. When should we solve problems? Should there be a specific time in the week? Where should we solve problems. Should we have a physical or virtual area where we all meet? And who should lead the problem-solving sessions? Is it always the same person or should we rotate who leads so that each of us can grow our leadership and facilitation skills? When embedding problem solving and continuous improvement, the behaviour of protecting the time is often far more important than using the 'right' tools and templates.

A foundry in one of the world's biggest aerospace companies implemented a simple discipline of bringing the team together once a week to focus on making things better. It was called 'Fix It Thursday' and two hours was allocated each Thursday afternoon to improvement activities. The agenda was loose – everything from quality concerns, to improvements to planning, from people's well-being to faulty tooling – and while an occasional tool or method was useful, the relentless focus on protecting that two hours a week was what really made the difference.

The question can be expanded to a wider scope:

'What are our standard ways to solve problems? Or to just improve things?'

In other words, not everything has to be a problem to get fixed. There are many situations where the current approach is working perfectly well but there is an even better, faster, more cost-effective way to do it. The methods in this fifth question work equally well for this situation.

3D uses three key problem-solving tools. They are simple, powerful and can be learnt in minutes. And they are free. The only cost is the time and commitment to make them a standard and to communicate to your colleagues along the following lines: 'It's a fact of life that in our daily work, we are continually facing problems and opportunities to improve. At the moment we do not have standard ways to engage together to make this happen. We make it up each time and everyone does it differently or it's just too difficult and we don't do it at all. We leave the problem in place and heroically work around it. This is a wasteful, inefficient and painful approach. To use an analogy, to make a train journey from A to B, we not only have to drive the train but we have to lay the tracks each time as well! It clearly makes good sense for us to have standard ways to engage together to fix problems so that, yes we need to make the train journey but the tracks are already in place. This doesn't cost more. It costs less. It doesn't take more time. It takes less time. We won't work harder. We'll work smarter. That's what we are going to do. We are going to learn three basic problem-solving tools that between them cover eighty per cent of the types of problem that we encounter in our daily work. We'll worry about the other twenty per cent later.'

The three problem-solving tools are:

- **Fishbone Diagram**

- **Five Whys**

- **A3 Problem Solving**

They can work on their own or they can work together. You'll be surprised at their simplicity. An advanced degree in statistical analysis is not required! Let's run through each in turn.

Fishbone Diagram

It's called a Fishbone Diagram because – well – it looks like a fishbone, with the head representing the problem and the fishbones representing possible categories of root causes. Typically there are six fishbones. Three on top and three on the bottom.

Here's how it works. The Fishbone Diagram is drawn on a whiteboard or flip chart with a circle for a head. The problem statement is written in the head, often framed as a 'Why?' question. A problem-solving group is formed of typically between three to six people. Between them they know all aspects of the problem.

They stand around the whiteboard and brainstorm possible root causes. There are different categorisations of root cause. Here are two common ones:

- **People, Process, Technology, Measures, Organisation, Environment.** This is my go-to categorisation. It works well in any environment.

- **Cluster into natural groupings.** Start brainstorming potential root causes and then cluster them into whatever categories you think make best sense.

There are a few ground rules. Think holistically. Let everyone have their turn and speak with no interruptions. Make sure you cover the full range of possible root causes. This is why the Fishbone Diagram is helpful. It helps the team think holistically.

A pharmaceuticals company was improving its product development process. This is an extremely complex process involving multiple teams, handovers and global round-the-clock time frames. There were many issues with the process. One of the biggest issues was conflicting data from multiple systems and no single source of the truth.

The improvement team of eight people were from different functions. Each had a different opinion on the causes of the conflicting data and who was at fault. People held strong opinions and feelings were running high. The group's communication was poor. There was more talking than listening. We decided to do a Fishbone Diagram. This proved to be the turning point and breakthrough in the initiative. The Fishbone Diagram provided the framework for the group's combined expertise to flow out and become the foundation for group understanding and communication. Time and again the group would return to their Fishbone Diagram to discuss one of the elements in more detail. It became the centrepiece of their visual display project area.

One of the sponsors said to me a few weeks later: 'For me, the Fishbone Diagram was the single most helpful thing that we have done in this initiative. It provided the glue for the group to stop finger pointing and understand that the problem had multiple causes and that the only way to solve it was as a team working together and making multiple small improvements. There was no single magic bullet. Now I have a whiteboard in my office with a blank Fishbone Diagram that we use whenever there's a tricky problem to discuss.'

This last point sums up why the Fishbone Diagram works so well. It gives the team a clear and collaborative framework for their discussion and into which to pour their combined expertise. It helps people frame their thinking and it helps people listen to each other. **Please see an example Fishbone Diagram in Figure 3.6**. The problem

5. What are our standard ways to solve problems?

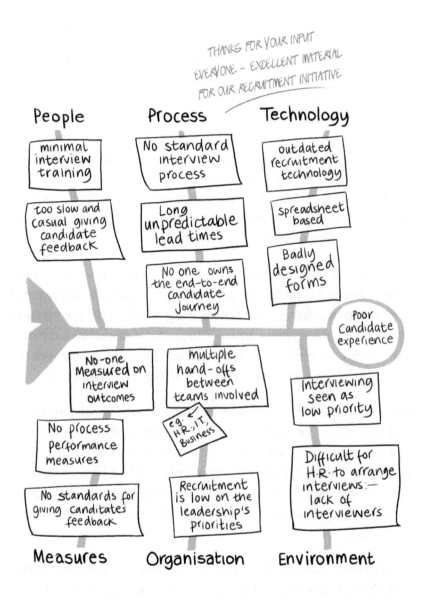

Figure 3.6 Fishbone Diagram example

is poor candidate experience. The Fishbone Diagram is being done as part of a wider initiative to improve the E2E recruitment process.

One of the pleasures of my work is sharing these tools and principles with people in everyday life situations. Let's finish this section with a recent example.

I was staying in a hotel in Birmingham. I returned to my room one evening to find that the room had been totally emptied by the cleaners, despite me having another night's stay booked, much to my surprise! I spoke to the front desk who quickly found my belongings, apologised, found me another room and offered me a free meal and drink for the inconvenience.

That evening I was chatting to the manager and asked if these sorts of mistakes had happened before and it turned out that this was not the only occurrence. He said he was going to talk to the cleaners and they would get a verbal warning. I suggested it might not have been their fault and asked if the hotel management had looked into the root cause of why these issues were occurring. They hadn't.

On the back of a menu, I sketched out and introduced him to the Fishbone Diagram tool to explore potential root causes. He was intrigued and discussed it the next morning with the team. That evening he told me that using the simple tool had been a real eye-opener. They had found an issue in how they communicated to the cleaning team which rooms were due to be empty. So it wasn't their fault at all!

It was a great example of W. Edwards Deming's famous quote: 'A bad system will beat a good person every time.' (Deming, W. E. 1993)[3]

Five Whys

This problem-solving method is asking the question 'why?' five times in order to get to the root cause of a problem. Asking 'why?' can be perceived as aggressive or rude. The Five Whys is effective, in part, because it gives everyone permission to ask the question not just once but multiple times without any negative feeling.

Here is a personal experience from a colleague to show the Five Whys in action.

Liam noticed the leaves on his recently planted plum tree were curling and turning brown, and no amount of water or food seemed to solve the problem. He asked himself:
- 'Why are the leaves curling?'

On closer inspection of the leaves it appeared that the tree was attracting aphids, which were drinking the sap from the tree and weakening it. Thinking he understood the problem, Liam enthusiastically applied aphid-killing insecticide to the leaves. However, after a few days the aphids would return, and he realised it wasn't sustainable to keep repeating this every few days.
- 'Why are the aphids returning to the tree?'

After some research it appeared that there was an absence of natural predators of aphids such as ladybirds.
- 'Why are there no ladybirds on the tree?

Further research showed that the ladybirds were being kept at bay by ants. It turned out that ants actually 'protect' the aphids from their predators and feed on the excess sap from the aphid, effectively 'farming' them.

In this moment, Liam knew he had found the root cause. He painted a band of thick ant-repellent paste around the base of the tree, blocking ants from accessing the tree. Within a few days, ladybirds were in abundance on the leaves, eating the aphids, and his fruit tree recovered.

You may have noticed that there are only three whys in this example. That's fine. The Five Whys is just a name. Use as many or as few whys as needed.

THE TEAM-BY-TEAM DIMENSION

In this next example the Five Whys helped resolve a problem that was both impacting outcomes and causing stress to everyone involved.

Sabine was the Head of Legal for an on-line retailer. She and her team were attending a 3D training session. She explained a particular frustration: 'The business doesn't understand how to use us effectively. We get all sorts of questions that have nothing to do with legal. Many of them concern commercial questions and just waste our time.' We decided to try using the Five Whys to find the root causes. We wrote down the issue on a flip chart as:

Issue: *Inconsistent and ill-defined interaction between legal and the business wasting time and causing poor service and frustration.*

*- **Why?** The legal team has never defined a consistent way for the business to use them effectively.*

*- **Why?** Because different people in the legal team respond to the same business request in different ways.*

*- **Why?** Because legal team members have come from a wide variety of backgrounds. This causes large variation in how they each respond to business requests. For example, some members of the legal team like to offer commercial as well as legal guidance; others prefer to stick to legal only.*

This thinking process, again after just three whys, caused a lightbulb moment for Sabine. She realised that the problem was as much with legal as with the business. Legal did not interact with the business in a standard way. There was variation based on the personal preferences of each lawyer. This variation was both invisible and random. In this situation, it was hardly surprising that interactions with the business were inconsistent, ill-defined and the cause of so much friction.

This realisation triggered the solution: legal ran an internal workshop to agree a set of principles on how they would interact with the business. This included a written guide to the business on 'Getting the best from your legal team!', followed up by a series of presentations and discussions. There was a short training programme for all members of the legal team to embed a new more consistent way of working.

A final note, there will be times when your answer to a why question splits into two or more paths. That's fine. Go down each path and see where each leads. Do whatever works. Have fun and enjoy the process.

A3 Problem Solving

A3 Problem Solving is so called because it uses the A3 paper size. It gives you a standard approach to problem solving that can include the Fishbone Diagram and Five Whys and is both simple and profound. Let's look at both these characteristics.

1. Why is A3 Problem Solving simple?

Because the headings and content on an A3 are straightforward and common sense. Here are typical headings on an A3 and good habits for completing them.

Title and team. Make the title meaningful and short. It should identify the issue to be solved in as few words as possible. The team should include the sponsor, the responsible leader and the core group needed to work with the responsible leader to make the A3 happen. The sponsor is someone with the authority to intervene as necessary to keep the A3 moving. Keep the core group as small as possible. Preferably between three to five people. Put a lot of thought into the team composition. Getting it right is a critical success factor to the A3 outcome.

Problem statement and current condition. Write as clearly as possible what the actual problem is. This usually takes a bit of reflection and thought. Don't worry. It doesn't have to be exactly right first time. Write down a first draft and then develop it as necessary and helpful. Start with the nature of the problem and then add what's happening at the moment. 'How often does it happen? When and where? How big is the problem? Is there a burning platform? Any immediate containment needed? What's its impact on customers, our people and cost?' Again, if the information isn't immediately available, don't worry. The initial draft is often a call to action to go and find it. Keep it as short and concise as possible while communicating the main points. It's better to be approximately right than precisely wrong. It might sound heresy to say it but for most problems it doesn't matter if it's happening twenty-nine or thirty-seven per cent of the time. It shouldn't be happening at all and we need to fix it!

Root cause. This is where you can use a Fishbone Diagram and Five Whys as part of your A3. There is a natural cascade as follows:

- Use the A3 to provide the improvement initiative framework.

- Use the Fishbone Diagram as your primary root cause problem-solving tool in the root cause section of the A3.

- Use Five Whys to drill down on individual elements of your Fishbone Diagram.

In practice you can use them in any way and any combination that you want. The above is a good starting point to build on. Root cause discussions often generate many potential solutions. Capture these as you go.

Goal and benefits. This section definitely takes some thought and reflection. We are good at pointing out problems. It's often a bit more difficult to say exactly what we'd like to happen. What would good look like? Or feel like? What's the outcome that we want? By when? What will the benefits be when we do achieve our goal? Impacting who? By how much? Again, the main thing is to make a start. Write a first draft and improve it from there. It's fine to put in estimates which you can refine as you go.

Solutions, implementation plan and follow-up. Our A3 gives us a solid foundation for generating solutions including a stockpile of good ideas from the discussions so far. 3D provides several ways for generating solutions which you can find in section: **E2E Q4: What is the new design to achieve our vision?** The implementation plan should have a timetable and contain the following elements: Owner? Team? Actions by when and by whom? How is it going? For simple solutions this may be all that's required. For more complicated solutions the team may want to consider some additional elements: Testing the solutions? Training required? Communications? Managing risks? You can find a comprehensive guide for testing solutions in section: **E2E Q5: How can we test and deploy our new design?**

The initial improvement is only the start. To keep it going, it's a good idea to make someone responsible for its performance and track how well it's working. This tracking might be a weekly update as part of the daily huddle on Monday. A good candidate for the job is the original A3 leader. This person cares about the problem and the solution and is naturally invested in its success.

Please see an example A3 in Figure 3.7. The problem is an increasing numbers of repeat calls into a service centre caused by a failure to resolve customers problems on the first call. Note the clarity and brevity that the A3 brings to improving this situation including two immediate calls to action.

85

Title: INCREASING REPEAT CALLS   **Date:** 17 June

Owner: Sara   **Team:** Belli, Wei, James

1. PROBLEM STATEMENT

Repeat contacts into the Service Centre have increased to 23% negatively affecting the customer and costing the business approx. $100,000 pa

2. CURRENT CONDITION

SOURCE	Call log
SAMPLE	03 Jan — 26 May
MEAN	(5 weeks) - 23%
TREND	Increasing

3. GOAL

To reduce the repeat call % to below 5% within 3 months of start of A3

4. ROOT CAUSES

- Lack of autonomy for service staff
- Coach support not sufficient
- Documents out of date

5. SOLUTION

- Increase staff authority levels
- Implement Skills Matrix and development plans
- Increase coach support for new starters

LET'S FAST FORWARD ON THESE TWO - BELLI

6. BENEFITS

- Better customer service $140,000 pa cost saving
- Increased employee satisfaction

7. IMPLEMENTATION PLAN

- Move authority to front-line to achieve one and done (Sara-July)
- Deliver the additional coaching and training required
- Create Skills Matrix and personal development plans

8. FOLLOW UP

- Track repeat call data on a weekly basis
  Track training and coaching executions

Figure 3.7 A3 Problem Solving example

2. Why is A3 Problem Solving profound?

Earlier I said that A3 Problem Solving gives an organisation a standard approach to problem solving that is both simple and profound. We've seen the simple characteristic in the above section. Here's why it is profound.

Provides a standard way. It provides a common language for people to engage together to solve problems or simply make something work better. Organisations often do not have this. There is no standard way for people to engage to solve small to medium problems. Organisations usually have a project management methodology but this tends to be most useful for heavyweight problems. There is often nothing for the small everyday problems within teams and between teams.

Develops skills and capabilities. Creating and delivering A3s develops individual skills in ways that people can use throughout their career. It develops ownership on behalf of the team. It is a real confidence booster when the problem is solved. Whatever job you do, it is a good skill to be able to clearly define a problem, understand what's happening at the moment, set the end goal and then make it happen.

Changes leadership behaviours. Instead of diving in with solutions and being the go-to firefighting experts, leaders can use A3s to develop and empower their people. And to develop their own leadership and coaching skills.

Keeps it real. A3s are short and to the point. There is nowhere to hide. You can read and understand an A3 in minutes. It is all on one page in front of you. Your eyes can flicker back and forth. 'What's the goal? Who's on the team? What are the issues? What's the plan? How's implementation going?' It's all there.

Drives action. A3s put the emphasis on doing and action. A3s create a culture of go see. If you want to get more detail, go and see for yourself. Go to where the work is. Talk to the people doing the work.

A3 Problem Solving has a deep and proven history. It initiated in the Japanese auto manufacturing industry where companies like Toyota are reputed to do around nine hundred thousand A3s each year! Imagine competing against this scale of relentlessness continuous improvement where every colleague in the business is trained and encouraged to identify improvement opportunities using the A3 approach. Each improvement is a raindrop and the raindrops create a torrent of improvement.

Retains knowledge. A3s make it easier to capture and retain knowledge and learnings in the organisation. They are easy to store, categorise and skim through. 'Before I start this initiative, I'll look through the other A3s we've done in similar areas this year.'

3. Making it real

Here's a case study of an organisation that has made A3s the foundation of their problem solving approach.

The leadership of a large services facility in Bangalore mandated the use of A3 Problem Solving. Other tools were recommended but optional. The use of A3s was not optional. When someone had a problem that was larger than a 'Just Do It', the first question that they were asked was: 'Can I see your A3?' The thinking was that most of their problems involved other teams in the business. The A3 provided a standard way for these teams to interact to fix problems. As one leader commented: 'The A3 replaces finger pointing with action.' While I was involved, the organisation averaged around two hundred and fifty A3s each year. They completed most of them using a three-to-six-week delivery drumbeat, depending on the size of the problem.

One example A3, that took five weeks, was improving taxi services to take staff home at night quickly, safely and economically. The centre worked in three shifts around the clock. Twenty-four hours a day, seven days a week. Many people had to use a taxi service to get home as public transport was not readily available. Everyone did their own thing. It was random. There were safety concerns. Delays with people often having to wait for an hour or more. Lots of taxi no-shows causing personal stress and issues at home. Overcharging and cost problems.

An A3 was launched. In five weeks, three taxi services had been selected based on service, reliability, quality and ease of ordering through mobile phones. A thirty per cent discount was negotiated based on volume. People got home more safely, quickly and economically.

This was one of those typical problems that is big enough to cause real issues but small enough to get ignored. This is A3 sweet spot and the A3 nailed it! What is interesting about this example is how everyday it is. It's not dramatic or huge or a strategic project. It is just continuously improving the little things that make a big difference.

This section: **What are our standard ways to solve problems?** has been a long one. That is deliberate. 3D embeds an engine of problem solving into the heart of your organisation. This section is that engine. We will see the principles contained in this section reflected in all three dimensions. Not just in Team-by-Team but also in End-to-End and Again-and-Again.

Benefits of Team-by-Team

There are profound benefits from a TBT way of working.

Happier customers. Each team and colleague has a laser focus on: Who are our customers? What do they want? How well are we doing? And how can we do better? This translates into happier customers. And happier customers translate into higher retention rates, increased revenues and lower costs.

Healthier working lifestyle. A certain amount of stress is inevitable in the workplace. It goes with the territory. The problem is that there is often a lot of unnecessary stress that can literally ruin people's working and personal lives. The key word is unnecessary. TBT ways of working target this unnecessary stress. Here are three examples:

- **Feeling powerless.** Living with the feeling that nothing ever gets better and it's impossible to change anything causes stress. TBT creates a culture where it is the expectation and norm to fix things. It provides the tools and capabilities to make it happen.

- **Doing low-value work.** Work that we know adds little or no value and is a waste of our time and expertise. This is disheartening as well as stressful. TBT targets and removes these activities.

- **Being overcapacity.** Up to our eyes with a workload that's impossible to achieve. Always being behind is stressful. TBT increases visibility and awareness of colleagues who are overcapacity and introduces a number of solutions.

We were making an internal communications video for a media company that had adopted 3D. Myra, one of the team leaders, was asked: 'Myra, what's changed for you since you moved to this new way of working?' Myra looked down. There was a long pause. It was obvious that whatever she was thinking was deeply moving for her. At last she looked up and replied. 'I enjoy coming to work again.' There was no more to be said.

Doing more with less. This takes many forms: reduced costs, higher productivity, additional capacity. Whatever the form, it comes down to doing more with less. Doing more of what our customers want and less of what they don't want. One word of caution. A knee-jerk reaction to freeing up capacity and higher productivity is to let people go. Don't do it. TBT isn't a once-off cost reduction programme. It's a cultural way of working based on respect for people. Keep this respect for people front of mind at all times. It will pay dividends many times over. *Let's say TBT gives you a thirty per cent productivity increase. Attrition is running at fifteen per cent so let's not replace people when they leave. Ten per cent of our workforce are contractors. Great, let's stop using them. The cost savings go straight to the bottom line. And let's use the remaining five per cent for personal development and problem-solving activities.*

Creating agility. There's more change coming faster than ever. And it's only going to accelerate. Having the speed and agility to handle this change is essential. Depending on project-based change used to work in the past. Now it's part of the answer but not the whole answer. Adopting a set of continuous improvement practices and principles provides the additional agility and speed that we need. This is the ultimate benefit of adopting the TBT way of working. Reacting to change and solving problems is just the way people work. You create an engine of change in your business.

Dealing with a crisis. People sometimes associate continuous improvement working practices with calm seas, steady as you go incremental improvements. But what happens in a crisis?

An engineering company was going through an invoice payables crisis, unable to pay suppliers with tens of thousands of unopened invoices across multiple factories and entities, amid significant organisation changes including a new finance system and outsource provider. Some suppliers had gone 'on stop' or were threatening to because of overdue payments, which meant global manufacturing sites had to stop production or shipment of flagship products. This included stopping the production line to avoid breaching health and safety.

The business had already adopted the TBT way of working. They now went into overdrive. Dedicated rooms were set up in each factory with visual management boards plastered on the walls including manual invoice burn-down charts and skills matrices to inform capacity balancing. They ran a twice-daily huddle in each room to align on priorities and assess progress. This kept heads above water and enabled rapid remediation of any suppliers going on stop. Separate teams were organised to focus on root cause analysis using a combination of Five Whys and A3s for the priority problems and to assign ownership for implementing the fixes.

By the end of month three, using TBT ways of working at full throttle, they had averted the crisis, resolved the root causes and moved back to business-as-usual operation.

Supporting innovative new tools. TBT provides a solid foundation on which to deploy innovations such as intelligent automation and remote working. These tools require continual tweaking and problem solving to realise their full potential and that's exactly what the TBT way of working provides.

The accounting function for a global real estate firm had embraced the TBT way of working. They liked the increased sense of purpose and improved culture across the site. Following the initial rollout, they were looking for further improvements and identified their current outsourcing arrangement as a constant source of frustration. It added twenty per cent to their cost base and caused constant errors and rework directly impacting clients and the in-house team.

It was decided to use automation to create an additional thirty per cent capacity equivalent to fifty people. This would enable cancelling the outsource agreement and moving the work back in-house. This would save the twenty per cent outsourcing cost, provide a better service to clients and offer more rounded and fulfilling work for the team.

It was a great plan on paper. The problem was that automating the work was much more difficult that originally envisaged because of the large amount of variation in the outsourced work combined with poor quality data. Fortunately, their TBT way of working came to the rescue. The ability of the teams to prioritise effectively, solve problems and work collectively combined with the reduction in hand-offs meant that they were still able to bring all the work back in-house. And once it was there they had more visibility of the issues and quickly set about resolving them, creating further improvements in client service and efficiency. They also enabled automation to work by removing unnecessary variation and improving data quality.

The sponsor summed up the final outcome: 'The project has been a success but it was a close call! We'd originally planned that automation alone would give us additional capacity of fifty people. In the end it gave us about fifteen people. Our TBT working environment gave us the remaining thirty-five.'

More fun. Yes fun! We're not robots, we're people. We enjoy having fun and we are more effective when we have fun. Use the time freed up by TBT ways of working to do new and creative activities that contribute to the team's success and are enjoyable.

---

1 Backaler, J. (2010, June 17). Haier: A Chinese Company That Innovates. Forbes.Com. https://www.forbes.com/sites/china/2010/06/17/haier-a-chinese-company-that-innovates/?sh=743b5ae85648

2 Aten, J. (2021, January). This Is Steve Jobs's Most Controversial Legacy. It Is Also His Most Brilliant. Inc.Com. https://www.inc.com/jason-aten/this-was-steve-jobs-most-controversial-legacy-it-was-also-his-most-brilliant.html

3 Deming, W. E. (1993, February). Deming Seminar [Presentation]. Deming Four Day Seminar, Phoenix, Arizona

Part Four

THE END-TO-END
DIMENSION

Everything of value is created by a process

- James Womack

End-to-End overview

The E2E dimension gives you a standard way to streamline and improve your end-to-end processes. There are five essentials that inform the E2E Five Questions Checklist:

1. Everyone involved knows who the customer(s) are and what they want. It starts and ends with the customer. A process can only perform well or badly in terms of what the customer wants. This is the customer purpose. Our measures on how well the process is performing should be based on this purpose. And our design should be based on delivering this purpose.

2. There is a good awareness of what's happening today. In particular, how capable is the current process in delivering what the customer(s) want? This is the essential background against which to design our new process. The current problems and opportunities are shared with everyone involved. This shared awareness is fundamental to any E2E improvement.

3. There's a shared vision for how the process should perform. This vision reflects what customers want from the process. Their purpose for using it. Making this vision happen is exciting and motivating for everyone involved. How the process is measured links directly back to the vision. There is a set of design principles that underpin this vision.

4. The new design delivers the vision. The team create a new design that delivers the vision and fulfils the customers' purpose. Sometimes it's transformational – sometimes it's incremental.

The team generates a wide range of potential solutions, so that many ideas are considered, before narrowing them down to the combination that best delivers the vision and reflects the agreed design principles.

5. There is a standard way to test, refine and implement the design. The reality is that almost no idea is completely right first time. The only way to really know is to test it. E2E takes an agile approach. It's iterative. This means there has to be a standard way to test and implement the new design.

These five essentials are the core of the E2E dimension. They give your organisation and people a standard way to engage together across different areas to streamline and improve your E2E processes.

Why End-to-End is important

The long-term success of an organisation depends on its processes working well. If processes are fragmented and broken, the ability to consistently win and delight customers and have a great work environment for staff is not possible. The key word here is consistently. The environment will be one of constant firefighting, frustration, stress and finger pointing. Having an effective way to continually improve end-to-end processes is not a nice to have, but a must-have. This is the purpose of the E2E dimension.

We often think of our organisations in terms of activities and functions. But customers couldn't care less about our activities and functions. Customers care about the value that we provide them. Whether it's through a product or service or both.

A customer of a technology company really values getting rapid and accurate sales quotations and then having the flexibility to change their mind about a few elements and get another quotation within the hour. They don't care that sales, product engineering, credit risk, pricing and legal all have to work as a well-oiled machine to make this happen.

It is a fact of life that processes are under constant attack and degradation from many types of change. Reorganisations, people, rules and regulations, policies, mergers and technology changes. These all have the potential to negatively impact the performance of processes. The people making the changes are often unaware of the negative impact they trigger.

For example, the head of compliance decides that all new credit applications, not just borderline cases, now require approval from legal. This makes perfect sense from their point of view. They have no awareness or visibility that this change adds five days to the time to get offers out, jeopardises meeting customer purpose, increases costs and stresses staff. It may still be a good decision but one that should be made with complete awareness.

Other factors add to the problem. Often no one owns or is measured on process performance. Or the wrong measures are used. Measures not linked to customer purpose but to functional targets. Driving wrong behaviours.

This is not all doom and gloom. In fact, it is massively positive. It's a fantastic opportunity. It means that organisations with a standard way for people to engage together to improve their E2E processes have a real advantage over those that don't. That's exactly what the E2E dimension provides.

End-to-End and Team-by-Team working together

Before diving into the detail of the E2E dimension, it's worth expanding on the synergies between TBT and E2E.

Many overlaps. All the tools and principles in TBT can be used in E2E improvements. There are many overlaps between the two dimensions. This is as you'd expect. After all, E2E is really just a series of teams working together – in sequence or in parallel – to generate value and outcomes for customers. For this reason and to avoid unnecessary duplication I refer back to the relevant TBT section when there is nothing extra to add for E2E. Just use the TBT tools and principles for these activities.

Special E2E principles and tools. At the same time, there are a series of tools and principles that are particularly helpful for E2E improvements. These are the focus of this section. Can these tools and principles also be used when appropriate in TBT situations? Absolutely. Use whatever you think will work best.

E2E is an essential addition. TBT is powerful and will make a rapid impact on your customers, your culture and your results. However, by itself it will ultimately stall as a single dimension. Why? This case study highlights the problem.

A global bank spent several years rolling out a Lean initiative using only a function by function (TBT) approach. The central improvement team would go into functions such as sales, service, operations and finance and using a rigid paint-by-numbers approach would run a series of Lean-type initiatives in the function. There was normally significant benefit in terms of saving costs and operating more efficiently. However, after several years the initiative stalled and was closed down. To quote one of the leadership team, 'It produced some good tactical results in the functions but ultimately it was a disappointment. We were hoping for transformational change in how we did business and this never happened.'

TBT by itself is not enough. Teams can optimise everything within their own gift. But much of their work and success will depend on the work of other teams. There has to be a standard and effective way for teams to engage together to continually improve their core processes. The processes that flow the value to your customers on whom the health and survival of your organisation depends. This is the rationale and power of the E2E dimension.

Special characteristics of End-to-End

There are some special characteristics of E2E improvements that are worth calling out.

Choose the right team. The success of your E2E improvement will depend – in large part – on the energy, enthusiasm, experience and combined expertise of the improvement team. The team needs to include someone from each function or team involved. This ensures that, between them, the team has a good working knowledge of what goes on in the process. Put a lot of value on experience, energy and enthusiasm. Do not accept the person who has just joined the organisation because they are available. Get the experts. Likewise, nothing will doom an E2E improvement faster than a cynical low-energy team.

There are some key roles to be allocated to the team members. The product owner will own the new design. The process architect will translate the new design into components to test and implement. And the improvement lead will manage the team through each stage of the E2E Five Questions Checklist.

The time commitment can be pragmatic and flexible. Colleagues from the main activity areas in the E2E process often commit at least fifty per cent of their time and are sometimes full time. Colleagues from the supporting functions are often nominated to be the point people for any interviews and working sessions. With no fixed time commitment.

Two other parties are often involved: customers and third-party suppliers. A *telecommunications and media company may use a third party to install cable and satellite TV dishes in homes. Attempting to improve the process without involving these third parties is a recipe for failure.* Indeed, many companies are reorganising themselves to better align their third parties to the processes they support.

Include policy in scope. It is important to keep policy in scope. In fact, that's an understatement. It is essential to keep policy in scope. Why? Because it's often conflicting, overlapping and ambiguous policies that are shredding the performance of an E2E process. If policy is taken out of scope, then in many cases it's not even worth trying. At every turn you'll be confronted with: 'Sorry, you can't change that, that's the policy!' In my experience, the word 'policy' is often used to excuse a multitude of sins. It can be a catch-all reason to avoid confronting problems. It's hard to argue against. Who's going to take on the sponsor when they say: 'Don't go there. That's a policy decision!' Or 'We can't implement that improvement. It's not aligned with policy.' Policy as a word sounds much grander than it actually is.

What is policy anyway? Wikipedia defines policy as: *'a deliberate system of principles to guide decisions and achieve rational outcomes.'* Against this definition it clearly makes sense to include policy in scope. A poorly performing process that is not meeting customer expectations, has multiple failure points and is stressing out staff is not achieving rational outcomes. It's achieving irrational outcomes!

At the same time, there is a natural sensitivity and caution towards changing policy. It's something that requires careful thought and planning. So what's the best approach? The good news is that there is an answer to this potential conflict area that has worked for me every time. Include in the charter wording to the effect of: 'Scope to include recommended improvements to policy.' This is a generally acceptable and non-threatening form of words that effectively puts policy in scope. It is all that is needed.

A global bank was improving its commercial lending process. Our sponsor, Zahra, was the head of global credit. Her initial reaction to putting policy in scope was to push back. Any policy changes in this bank were super sensitive. I explained why it was so important and she agreed to the wording for the scope to include 'sensible recommendations to streamline policy'.

The mix of policies in this bank was very complicated. The reason was that there were so many different categories of policy. Regional Policy. Product Policy. Credit Policy. Industry Policy. Money Laundering Policy. Fraud Policy. The list went on! They had all been drafted by different people with no visibility of the impact of their policy on the overall mix. Each set of policies made good sense within their own category but no one had the remit or visibility of the overall picture.

Zahra led a dedicated stream of activity to streamline policy. She didn't delegate this. She did it herself. The team made many improvements to policy. Some were minor tweaks. Others had immediate global impact. Some years earlier it had been decided that every country, where the client and the bank both had an office, needed to sign off on new loans. Even though the loan was being arranged in Head Office and there was no value in this local sign-off. It wasn't unusual for twenty or more local country signatures to be required. For no good reason. It was just the policy. This caused large delays of weeks and months in loans being approved. And a lot of unnecessary work and rework. This policy was scrapped. Gone. That one change alone had a huge impact on customer service, speed and impact. Zahra's decision and active participation in putting policy in scope was a game changer!

Stakeholder engagement is key. By its nature, an E2E improvement involves multiple parties and it is easy to overlook someone. It's not just the core teams and functions involved. Other parties could include support teams such as IT, finance and HR. Specialist teams like procurement, compliance, legal and audit. External parties such as suppliers, intermediaries and the customers of the process. Always ask yourself: 'Is there anyone I'm not talking to who could pop up in a few weeks and say, "Hold on, I never agreed to this initiative and these changes. Stop everything now!"'

Know the dance steps. Improving processes is not difficult but you do need to know the choreography. The dance steps and the right order of those steps. For example, it's important to understand what's happening today before designing for tomorrow. There is often pressure to skip this step. It almost always backfires. Go slow to go fast.

A senior executive at a global services company was giving a speech to his team. I was part of the audience. 'We've just lost a large sale involving many different parts of our organisation. The reason is because of the time we took to get our bid to the client and to respond to requests for changes. I've had one of my people look at our bid process and they've told me that there are sixteen different approvals required in this process. That's way too many. I've told them to reduce that by half. And I've asked for the solution on my desk within two weeks!'

Sounded good – the problem was that the dance steps were all wrong. He was jumping straight to a solution. Too many approvals is usually a symptom of a poor process, not the root cause. Sure enough, after a few instant solutions that didn't work, the process was still broken and the executive's focus moved on to new things. In fact, things were worse because people got the feeling that this would never be fixed. Too difficult. Just keep on walking through honey with flippers on.

The charter is a must-have. The initial improvement usually starts as a project and then evolves into continuous improvement.

This means that having a charter is a must-have. It is your compass and keel. It guides the direction. It provides the stability through inevitable choppy waters. It's the go-to document for any questions on background, context, benefits, risks, team and timescales. It supports having the difficult conversations up front.

Writing a charter

Start your E2E improvement with a simple one-page charter. Keep it to one page. Less is more. Writing the first draft of an E2E charter can usually be done in an hour or less. It is a living document. It does not have to be perfect first time. In fact, it never will be. The typical sections are: Charter Name, Goals, Target Benefits, Team, Start Date and Timeline, Risks and Issues.

Please see an example charter for transforming an E2E Recruitment Process in Figure 4.1. The sponsor has highlighted the number one objective from her perspective.

The charter helps crystallise some important considerations.

Confirms the dedicated team. The charter confirms the improvement team members, their roles and their time commitment. No grey areas. No misunderstandings. It's there in the charter.

Clarifies the scope. I recommend starting with a larger rather than smaller scope. It opens up bigger opportunities. This is somewhat counter-intuitive. People associate large scope with increased risk and small scope with reduced risk. E2E scope can be the opposite. A larger scope avoids the situation where the upstream function is causing all the problems for downstream functions but is out of scope of the improvement.

An engineering company had launched an improvement initiative for its operations function. Unfortunately, the sales and service functions who created most of the work for the operations team were

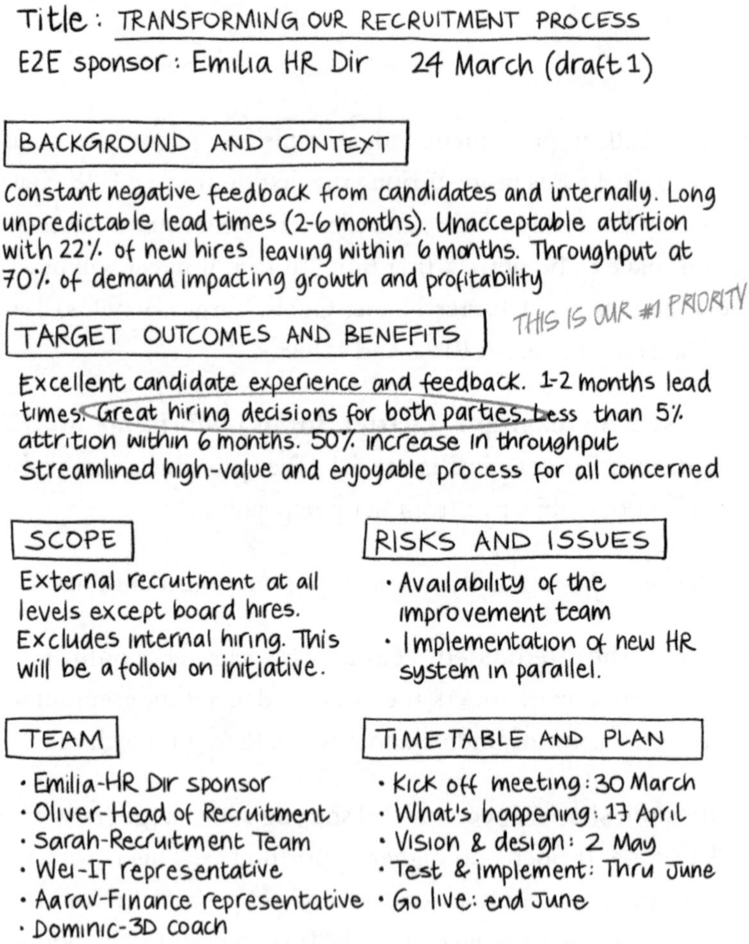

Title: TRANSFORMING OUR RECRUITMENT PROCESS

E2E sponsor: Emilia HR Dir   24 March (draft 1)

BACKGROUND AND CONTEXT

Constant negative feedback from candidates and internally. Long unpredictable lead times (2-6 months). Unacceptable attrition with 22% of new hires leaving within 6 months. Throughput at 70% of demand impacting growth and profitability

TARGET OUTCOMES AND BENEFITS   THIS IS OUR #1 PRIORITY

Excellent candidate experience and feedback. 1-2 months lead times. Great hiring decisions for both parties. Less than 5% attrition within 6 months. 50% increase in throughput Streamlined high-value and enjoyable process for all concerned

SCOPE

External recruitment at all levels except board hires. Excludes internal hiring. This will be a follow on initiative.

RISKS AND ISSUES

- Availability of the improvement team
- Implementation of new HR system in parallel.

TEAM

- Emilia-HR Dir sponsor
- Oliver-Head of Recruitment
- Sarah-Recruitment Team
- Wei-IT representative
- Aarav-Finance representative
- Dominic-3D coach

TIMETABLE AND PLAN

- Kick off meeting: 30 March
- What's happening: 17 April
- Vision & design: 2 May
- Test & implement: Thru June
- Go live: end June

Figure 4.1 E2E Charter example

out of scope. In fact, the heads of sales and service were adamant that their teams were not to be 'disrupted' by the initiative. The results were disappointing. Most of the operations workload was rectifying problems originating in the sales and service functions. There were a few tactical improvements in how this failure demand was handled but no analysis of what was causing it or reduction in the workload itself. Restricting the scope had hamstrung the initiative.

In the above example it would have been good to have a larger scope from a length perspective. More functions included in the end-to-end process. It works equally well to have a larger scope from a breadth perspective. More participants in each function. This case study demonstrates the point.

The trading arm of a food manufacturing conglomerate was streamlining its counterparty onboarding process. This is a key process which when working well means that new counterparties are onboarded quickly thus enabling more trading activity. The current process was rife with delays, rework and long, unpredictable lead times.

There were six trading desks each trading a different food commodity. The initial scope was to look at the flow of work from just one trading desk all the way through the process to – in the words of the sponsor – 'save time and effort'. After working through E2E Question Two: 'What is happening today?' it was clear that the core process itself was working fine. The root causes of the problems were how they prioritised work through the process (or didn't!) and the capacity constraints within credit and legal where work got stuck and went into a black hole. We proposed to the sponsor to expand the scope to incorporate all six trading desks. This would allow us to see the total demand flow and address the capacity and prioritisation issues. The sponsor agreed and the scope was expanded.

One proviso to this think-big principle: get approval in advance to shrink the scope if new learnings from the improvement suggest this is a good idea.

Acknowledges other projects. Acknowledge other projects in the risks and issues section. An E2E process will almost always have other projects and improvement activity going on in it. It may be a new workflow project. A reorganisation of one of the teams. A better reporting system. The leaders of these initiatives should be viewed as stakeholders of the E2E improvement. It's important to get them on board. My experience is that they are supportive when they are briefed in advance – potential detractors when overlooked.

Sets out the timeline. It might be eight or twelve weeks or sixteen weeks. Whatever makes sense. My view is take more rather than less time. What's important is to end up with an effective and streamlined process that's going to delight your customers for years to come.

Recognises the risks and issues. There will always be risks and issues. The important thing is to acknowledge them. By putting them on the table you are able to plan for them and mitigate as possible.

Don't be afraid to pivot. The charter is a living document. Its purpose is to represent the best way forward based on latest information. It's not set in stone. Use your charter to reflect new information as it becomes available and agree to sensible changes in direction with your stakeholders.

End-to-End Five Questions Checklist

Here is the E2E Five Questions Checklist. There is a well-proven logic to the order of these steps. As a general rule, it is best to follow the order. At the same time be pragmatic and flexible. If you discover a no-brainer opportunity during Question One that can be quickly implemented at little or no cost, go right ahead.

1. **Who are our customers and what do they want?**

2. **What is happening today?**

3. **What is our vision for tomorrow?**

4. **What is the new design to achieve our vision?**

5. **How can we test and deploy our new design with agility?**

E2E is simple and common sense just like TBT. There is nothing complicated. There are some innovative tools which we'll explore in the following sections, but they are not difficult to use. Each tool can be used with a whiteboard, Post-it notes and Sharpie pens. Each of the Five Checklist Questions is explored in detail in the following sections. Let's go!

1. Who are our customers and what do they want?

Plus the same two follow-up questions that we used in TBT: **How do we prioritise them? And how do we measure our performance?**

We start at exactly the same place as the TBT initiative. With the customer. There is only one reason for our process to exist. To meet the needs of our customers.

One special note. You might be thinking: Is this exactly the same as the TBT first question? The answer is it's similar but different. The TBT first question is asking: 'Who are the customer(s) of the team?' The E2E first question is asking: 'Who are the customer(s) of the process?' There are many overlaps in the answers to the two questions. This section will focus on the points that are particularly relevant to E2E improvements.

1. Who are our customers and what do they want?

E2E processes almost always have more than one type of customer. I have been in many workshops where the question 'Who is the customer of this process?' consumed hours of debate and argument. The assumption behind this question is that there is a single customer for a process. It is usually a false assumption.

A life and pensions company was improving its sales process. We were working through this first question. The going-in assumption by the attendees was that there was just one customer type. This generated a heated discussion with some participants arguing that 'Of course our customers are the brokers who represent our products. If we don't keep them happy then we don't have a business!' Other participants argued that the policy holders must be the real customers. 'After all, they are the end consumers.'

The concept of multiple customer types came to the rescue. By the end of the session there was clarity and agreement that there were three types of customer. The end consumer who wants good value and dependable life insurance and pensions. The broker who wants to win and retain end consumers with good products, earn a healthy commission and receive fast and efficient service. The organisation that needs to meet market expectations in terms of growth, profit and sustainability.

The next step is to determine what each customer type wants from the process. What is their underlying purpose? We looked at three ways to find out what customers want in the TBT dimension: watch them, ask them and anticipate them. These three ways work equally well in E2E improvements. Please refer to section: **TBT Q1: Who are our customers and what do they want?**

An accurate understanding of customer purpose can lead to transformational results.

The same life and pensions company had an iconic brand dating back two hundred years to the Napoleonic wars and beyond. In other words, they had been paying out life insurance claims for more than two hundred years. They'd definitely know what their customers wanted. Right? Not entirely.

The claims process was based on the assumption that customers wanted to get the life insurance sum paid as quickly as possible. The process had been designed on this basis. Including the need to guard against fraud. So the process was top heavy with checks and approvals and more checks and approvals. The customers were asked for copious amounts of documentation and proof before any action could be taken. Emphasis on 'any action'.

There were endless circles of requests, wrong and missing information sent in, followed by more requests, followed by chasers. It was an email and paper snowstorm. Made worse when management decided on a blitz to reduce the backlog. Then it became a blizzard! The average lead time from request to pay out was seventy-eight days – or four months – with large variability and unpredictability. The ratio of value to failure demand was about thirty per cent. In other words, for every value interaction such as a 'there's been a death in my family and I'd like to make a claim please' there were three failure interactions such as 'I don't understand your claim form' or 'I can't find my aunt's birth certificate' or 'why has no one called me back?'

There was an eight strong management team to manage the people who actually did the work. These colleagues – the people at the front line – had no discretion or decision-making power.

As always, we started off by exploring customer purpose. To everyone's surprise, the customer purpose was subtly different from the current understanding. There were three main customer purposes:

- Advice on next steps and what to do.

- Needing an immediate advance of around five thousand pounds to cover the funeral costs.

- Investment advice on what to do with the life insurance money.

In very few cases did the customer want payment of the full amount of money as soon as possible. We also analysed the number of fraud cases. Far fewer than the common perception. The management system was based on a misunderstanding of the customer purpose and triggered an avalanche of failure demand and unhappy customers as a result.

The solution was rapid and transformational. Five of the eight managers moved to other roles. Costs were reduced by twenty per cent. Colleagues on the front line were authorised to make payments of up to six thousand pounds for funeral expenses immediately on the first customer call and on their own judgement. The process was redesigned to make it easier to provide the required documentation. Lead times halved and with minimal variation. Customer satisfaction went up and failure demand went down. All triggered by a clearer understanding of what customers actually wanted.

2. How do we prioritise them?

This question is fundamental to successful E2E design. Yet it is often missed. Processes almost always have three or four or five different types of customer. You can't keep everyone happy all the time! Choices need to be made. The important thing is to have the discussion. To make the prioritisation decisions. And to design the process based on those decisions. This customer prioritisation is an important intersect of E2E improvements with strategy.

Going back to the life and pensions company improving its sales process. The discussion recognised that, historically, the prioritisation had been the broker first, the organisation second and the end consumer third. This prioritisation had many strategic implications including product design, end consumer value proposition, pricing, broker commissions and multi-channel strategy.

This E2E improvement generated both an improved selling process and a strategic review of customer prioritisation. This led to a series of initiatives aimed at building closer relationships with the end consumers.

This story shows why E2E process improvements must have senior sponsorship. The sponsor and product owner, together with other leaders, need to make these prioritisation decisions. How customers are prioritised directly impacts the new design.

3. How do we measure our performance?

This is the same question that we asked in TBT but with a difference. In TBT it is just one team choosing the measures. In an E2E there will be multiple teams. So not only can they be using the wrong measures, they can also each be using different measures. The potential to use measures that drive the wrong behaviours, not aligned to meeting customer purpose, is even greater.

A financial services organisation had recently launched a new equity release product. It was targeted at older adults who owned their own home, had significant equity in it and could benefit from releasing some of that equity as cash. They were improving the E2E sales process, from initial interest to fulfilment. There were three teams in the E2E sales process.

- *The marketing team who were responsible for the website design. They were measured on the number of hits on the website and people expressing an interest and requesting a callback.*

- *The call centre colleagues who were responsible for making these calls and turning them into requests for a meeting. They were measured on the number of meetings that they set up for advisors.*

- *The sales advisors who were responsible for meeting prospects at their home, making the sale and converting them into customers. They were measured on the number of sales that they made.*

While answering E2E Checklist Question Two: What is happening today? we discovered that the E2E process performance had serious problems. Many of the people attracted by the website and requesting a callback were not right for the product. Over ninety per cent of the meetings arranged for the advisors by the contact centre colleagues turned out to be a waste of time, both for the potential customer and the advisor. And over twenty per cent of the sales made by the advisors were cancelled a few weeks later when the customers changed their minds during the statutory cooling off period.

The root cause was that each team was measured on different things and none of the measures related to customer purpose! Customers didn't care how many hits there were on the website. Or how many appointments were set up. Or how many sales were made. All that a customer cared about was buying a product that genuinely benefited them and made a positive difference, financial and otherwise, to their life. Yet each team was behaving with perfect logic based on how they were being measured.

The main improvement was to implement a common set of measures across the E2E process directly related to customer purpose. Each team was measured on the same things. The measures adopted were:

- *Customer satisfaction*

- *Total number of sales with high customer satisfaction*

- *Percentage of advisor meetings that turned into sales*

Positive results started to come through within weeks. Sales, customer satisfaction and the percentage of successful advisor meetings all started tracking upwards. The teams were now working together on a daily basis, constantly tracking these three metrics and adjusting web design, calling scripts and face-to-face sales approaches to optimise the overall performance.

Understanding customer purpose and using measurements related to customer purpose can be useful in all walks of life, not just work.

A friend's daughter found learning the piano tiresome as she was told she had to practise for two hours a week around her one hour of lessons a week. He set her the new goal to say that she could practise as much or as little as she liked as long as she met the incremental goals set by her teacher. The change of focus was now not about clockwatching to 'make up the time' but about developing to meet the next goal, whether that took twenty minutes or four hours across the week.

His son had the lucky job of being responsible for stacking the dishwasher, which he disliked as he was constantly told off for 'doing it wrong' and 'taking too long'. He and his wife changed their approach to say that the goal was that dishes need to come out clean no matter how they were stacked (they stopped telling him 'how' to load the dishes) – it was his responsibility to coordinate that for the house and if he improved things then he would get a treat. His motivation changed and after trying different ways of loading the dishwasher to get the best results he was the one telling the family they were stacking it the wrong way!

Answering E2E Checklist Question One provides the bedrock for our E2E improvement. We've identified the customer types, found out what they want, prioritised them for our design decisions and adopted measures based on what they want. We now have a solid foundation to build on.

2. What is happening today?

How well is our process meeting its customer purpose? Where is the waste? Where are the issues and opportunities?

To answer this question we use a combination of four tools:

• **SIPOC**

• **Value Stream Mapping**

• **Information Elements**

• **Mississippi Chart**

The different perspectives that they provide give us deep insight into not only what is happening today but – just as importantly – how to transform our E2E process for tomorrow.

SIPOC

SIPOC (pronounced 'Cy-poc') is an acronym for Suppliers, Inputs, Process, Outputs, Customers. I wouldn't leave home without it! It's my go-to tool to kick off any process improvement. It's simple to use, asks the right questions and generates insight in minutes. Who are the suppliers of the process? What are the inputs? How big is the scope in terms of process steps? What are the outputs? Who are the customers? SIPOC triggers the right discussions on these questions and enables rapid iterations and learnings.

Here's how it works. I always use Post-it notes and Sharpie pens so that changes are easy to make. Write Suppliers, Inputs, Process, Outputs and Customers on five Post-it notes. Put these in a row at the top of your whiteboard or wall. Then start with Process. Brainstorm the high-level activity blocks in the process and put these underneath the Process Post-it. You'll find this immediately generates a great discussion on the scope. Where it starts. Where it ends. What's in between. Keep it high level. Don't get too granular. Aim for around five to ten process steps. The Post-it notes allow you to make rapid changes and additions.

Then move to Customers. Who are the different types of customer for the process and what is their relative priority? We know this from E2E Checklist Question One. Write each customer type on their own Post-it note and put them in descending order of priority. Finally, work through Suppliers, Inputs and Outputs.

Why start with Process and Customers? Why not just work left to right? This case study helps explain.

I spent two years in Africa leading the Lean deployment of a financial services organisation. During that time we did over thirty E2E improvements, touching just about every core process in the organisation including sales, service, new product development, operations, HR, IT and finance. We started each initiative by building a SIPOC with the sponsor of each process and their team. Normally on their office wall or whiteboard. We put Suppliers, Inputs, Process, Outputs and Customers Post-its on the wall and followed the steps above for Process and Customers. It always worked – there was always a good discussion. By the end of the meeting we had the scope agreed, the process steps we needed to explore, confirmation of the types of customer and the sponsor's view on their relative importance. We also had the names of people who were experts in each process step. Time and again we'd use the outputs of this short meeting as our stake in the ground on scope, customer prioritisation and the improvement team members. All in sixty minutes or less. We left Suppliers Inputs and Outputs for a follow-up meeting with the team involved.

Please see an example SIPOC for making a cup of tea in Figure 4.2. Even this simple example triggers all sorts of questions. Who are the Customers of the process? Should sweetener be included in the Suppliers? Is adding the teabag, milk, sugar and stirring one or more steps?

Value Stream Mapping

I like to visualise Value Stream Mapping as a sort of super powerful vacuum cleaner! It literally lets you vacuum up the process from beginning to end, capturing the key information as you go. The activities. The teams. The technology. The lead times. The process times. The issues and the opportunities. It is also well received by the people doing the work. It's often the first time they have ever been asked in detail what they do and their ideas for improving what they do. To repeat a favourite saying of mine: 'The people who do the work are the people who know how to make the work work better.' The Value Stream Mapping activity recognises this truth and is based on respect for people doing the work and their passion and expertise.

1. How Value Stream Mapping (VSM) works

Value Stream is another term for an end-to-end process. Literally a stream of value. There are many variations of VSM. The 3D approach is to keep things as simple as possible. The VSM team comprises one person from each area involved in the process. They walk the process and complete the VSM as a team. So representatives from all the areas involved are seeing the E2E process as a team. Usually for the first time. They meet with the people who do the work at each stage and ask a series of questions.

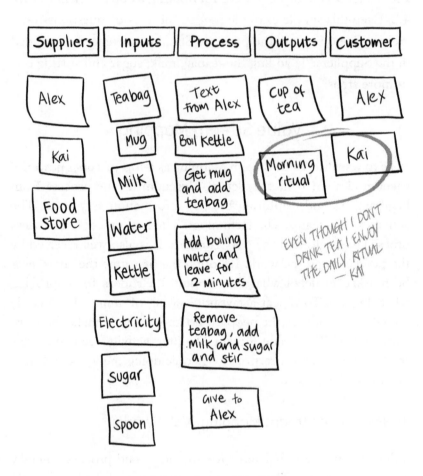

Figure 4.2 SIPOC example

- What's the work coming into your team?

- What are the volumes and variations?

- What are the activities you do?

- What are the lead and process times for each activity?

- What IT systems do you use?

- What capacity do you have for each activity?

- What are the issues and problems that you experience?

- What are the opportunities for improvement that you see?

- Can I just observe you and the team doing these activities to get a good understanding?

Please see an example of a completed VSM template for Step One of an E2E Recruitment Process in Figure 4.3. Issues and opportunities are often captured on separate pages not shown here. You can download a set of Value Stream Mapping templates at **the3dworkplace.com**.

The output is a Value Stream Map with the completed templates running horizontally across the wall. You can see the whole process at a glance. It is a highly visible, easy to understand representation of what is actually happening in the process: the steps, the technology, the lead times, the time spent doing value-add work – and non-value-add work. The information flows, the approvals, the rework flows and how often things go wrong. These Value Stream Maps are usually hand drawn and can often take up a whole wall.

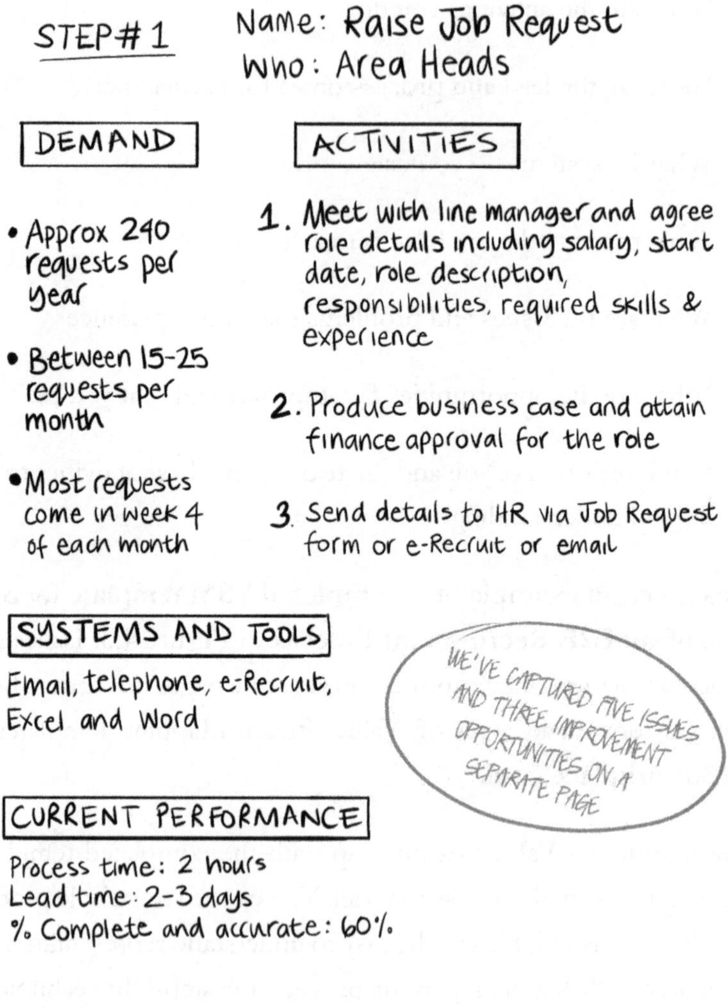

STEP # 1

Name: **Raise Job Request**
Who: **Area Heads**

DEMAND

- Approx 240 requests per year

- Between 15-25 requests per month

- Most requests come in week 4 of each month

ACTIVITIES

1. Meet with line manager and agree role details including salary, start date, role description, responsibilities, required skills & experience

2. Produce business case and attain finance approval for the role

3. Send details to HR via Job Request form or e-Recruit or email

SYSTEMS AND TOOLS

Email, telephone, e-Recruit, Excel and Word

WE'VE CAPTURED FIVE ISSUES AND THREE IMPROVEMENT OPPORTUNITIES ON A SEPARATE PAGE

CURRENT PERFORMANCE

Process time: 2 hours
Lead time: 2-3 days
% Complete and accurate: 60%

Figure 4.3 VSM Template example

2. Value Stream Mapping characteristics

The VSM has several characteristics that make it excellent at building understanding with everyone involved on what's happening at the moment. And pointing the way to possible solutions.

Shows the big picture. The VSM is a visible and easy to understand representation of what's happening on the ground. It means that the stakeholders can see the big picture together. And understand it together. This last point is important. Before developing our new design we need to get our colleagues on the same page in terms of what's happening now. The VSM is a great communication tool.

Generates discussion. The VSM generates constructive discussion between the teams and areas involved. It provides a framework for collegiate and pragmatic thinking. If a percentage is wrong, then pick up a Post-it note, write the correct number and move on. If a stakeholder disagrees with something, thank them for their input, write it down on a Post-it and stick it on the VSM. This simple action has three effects. It acknowledges their point. Captures it. And provides a marker for action. It evaporates finger pointing and the blame game. 'We're all one team. Let's just fix this thing.'

Builds credibility. The colleagues from each area are reporting as a team to the leaders of each area. This may well be a first! It gives credibility to the information that it is coming from the people who are actually doing the work. It provides an open and informed forum for all relevant topics – including political hot potatoes – to get discussed and addressed.

Encourages action. Decisions get made fast. The decision makers are seeing the VSM as a group. The people who do the work are presenting the VSM as a group. Remember the saying from TBT: 'See together, know together, act together.' Well, the VSM is exactly the same. It's a call to act together. I've been at many VSM group meetings where decisions that had been bouncing around email inboxes for weeks and months got made in minutes. It was suddenly obvious to everyone involved what was the right thing to do.

Dissolves silo thinking and behaviour. It becomes one group of human beings: the improvement team of people who do the work, recommending to another group of human beings – the leadership team – on how to make things work better. People often ask me ahead of launching an E2E improvement: 'Shouldn't we have some preliminary meetings to address our silo-based thinking problem?' My answer: 'Absolutely not. It will start to dissolve as a natural part of the improvement approach.' The VSM is a silo solvent!

Creates lightbulb moments. The VSM creates those special lightbulb moments when the penny drops and everyone involved suddenly get it. One way to switch the lights on is to call out the total lead time and total process time in the E2E process: 'So to summarise we are taking forty-five days to do six hours work! And remember, no one puts time into a process on purpose. Long lead times are an indication of waste.' This perspective of comparing the lead time to the process time, in this case taking forty-five days to do six hours work, really hits home with people. One follow-up question I often ask is: 'So why can't we take six hours to do six hours work?' The reality is that it's not usually possible but it's a great question to ask.

Builds the foundation for our new design. People sometimes challenge the necessity to do all this work on what's happening at the moment. They ask: 'Why don't we just move to creating the new design?' The answer is that the VSM and the other tools in this section make the new design easier to develop. Much easier! And more robust in terms of what will work and what will not work. It can generate a series of quick wins that would otherwise be missed. Sometimes I will stare at a VSM by myself and in silence. It sounds a bit out there but it often starts talking to me. The new design can be obvious as a result of the effort put in at this stage.

Please see an illustration of a VSM team in action in Figure 4.4. How many of these characteristics can you see in the illustration?

3. Value Stream Mapping in action

Value Stream Maps have a certain informality that makes it easier to share and discuss sensitive issues. Their large size also makes it possible for a group of people to see the big picture together.

Case study one: Sensitive issues

A pharmaceuticals company was improving its 'Request for Service' process. The sponsor was the CIO. He was a highly authoritarian, somewhat intimidating figure. People were scared of him. The culture was very formal. All last names. No first names.

There were over one thousand requests per month for new IT-related services. Hardware, software, upgrades, networks. The process was fragmented and slow with lots of rework and finger pointing. Users were unhappy. The CIO was getting heat from his peers. The Value Stream Map showed eighteen steps in the process where people had expected about eight and an astonishing number of approvals required – fourteen! So many in fact that we'd developed a new visual icon just to represent approvals. And most of them came late in the process which carries its own inefficiencies.

The CIO exploded when he saw the number of approvals. 'This is ridiculous!' he exclaimed. 'Who ordered all these approvals?' There was an awkward silence and then a junior member of the improvement team replied, 'Well, actually sir, I think that you did. We discovered that many times when things went wrong, the CIO office would request a new approval be put in place. And they've just built up over time.'

Figure 4.4 VSM Team in action

There was a stunned silence and then the CIO started laughing. 'Good point,' he replied. 'Well I asked for them to go in and now I'm asking them to go out. Please do a new design that has the minimum number of approvals required and no more. Don't involve people if they don't need to be.' The team breathed a collective sigh of relief and the scene was set for a transformational new design. But imagine sending an email to the CIO office or preparing a PowerPoint with the same message. High risk and probably not a pleasant experience.

Case study two: Sharing the big picture

A consumer products company was a few weeks into a 3D pilot. We were sharing 'what is happening today?' for the order to cash process. It was a large room. The Heads of Finance, IT and Marketing were present plus some twenty process stakeholders. The current state was extremely fragmented with over sixty issues. The Value Stream Map had over twenty-five process steps and sixty issues highlighted in red. It was handwritten and about fourteen feet long and six feet high. Many functions were involved across several geographies. Finance and Service in Poland. Sales in France. Supply Chain in Ireland. Information Technology in the UK.

The change team was talking the leaders of these areas through the whole end-to-end situation. Light bulbs were going off all over the room. Sacred cows were being openly discussed and challenged for the first time. The conversation was crisp and constructive. There was no finger pointing. The Value Stream Map made it obvious that problems in one area usually had their originations in other areas. At the end of the session the Head of Finance said to the improvement team: 'You've started something very big around here. I'm sponsoring a half-day briefing session with the Board next month.' It was the start of a global 3D roll-out.

Information Elements

When we think about a process, a natural first reaction is to think about it from an activities perspective. However, what can be just as important are the information elements involved in the activities. Activities in a process are often relatively simple. The complexity can lie in the information elements underneath the activities.

1. What is an Information Element and how does the analysis work?

Information Elements can be abbreviated to INFELS. It is a powerful tool and perspective with which to redesign and transform processes. When we share INFELS analysis with a client for the first time the reaction is often: 'I wish I'd known about this earlier. It explains so much in terms of why we've struggled in previous initiatives. We didn't have this view.'

What is an INFEL? It is a high-level piece of information used in the process. So an address is an INFEL. The street number is not an INFEL It's too granular. It might be useful as a data element for programming purposes but not as an INFEL for improving the process.

INFELS analysis is a three-step process:

1. List the INFELS behind each activity.

2. Select a lens through which to view the INFELS.

3. Improve both the activities and the INFELS based on that lens.

There are many lenses that you can apply to INFELS analysis. Failure impact, combination, cost, effort, timing and predictability are some of the most useful ones. A few case studies will bring the concept to life and demonstrate why it is such a powerful improvement tool.

2. INFELS lenses in action

Failure impact. This lens looks at the failure impact of an INFEL having a wrong value based on three criteria:

- How severe is the impact if the value is wrong?

- How likely is it to be wrong?

- How frequently is a bad value occurring?

If all three are high scores then clearly there is a big failure impact.

A utility provider wanted to improve its core operational processes. There were sixteen processes in scope. For example, taking a meter reading or change of tenancy. We did an INFELS analysis and identified forty-three INFELS involved in the sixteen processes. We then applied a failure impact lens to each INFEL and identified five INFELS that, if the value was wrong, had exceptionally high failure impact. A prime example was an incorrect meter reading. This one INFEL impacted ten of the sixteen core processes and – with a wrong value – triggered multiple types of waste and bad customer experience.

The solution was to assign dedicated teams to clean up each of the five INFELS. Their objective was to find new ways to make sure that these INFELS always had correct values. The teams reduced the percentage of incorrect values by over seventy per cent in four weeks using simple innovations such as asking the customer to take photographs of the meter with their mobile phones.

In this example improving the processes had little to do with the activities and everything to do with the INFELS behind the processes.

Combination. This lens looks at the optimum combination of INFELS to make the process as streamlined and effective as possible.

A global bank was improving its lending process to corporate clients. The process was relatively simple from an activity viewpoint:

- *Understand the client need*

- *Evaluate the client's situation and credit worthiness*

- *Make a lending decision*

- *Pay the money*

However, beneath the surface it was a massively complicated, lengthy and fragmented process. The client requirement was for a lending decision in a month or less. They had a business to run. In practice it was taking anywhere up to three months. And the process was opaque and unpredictable. The client received little insight into how the lending decision was progressing. Sometimes to receive bad news at the last minute.

The main cause of long lead times was the large amount of information that had to be collected and processed. We identified sixty-two INFELS involved in a lending decision. Example INFELS included company details, profitability, lending track record, analyst report, industry sector rating, country rating, subsidiary sign-offs and multiple approvals. Imagine sixty-two of these and you can see that what looked like a simple process from an activity perspective becomes a very complicated process from an INFELS perspective. The biggest problem with the current process was that it didn't adapt to handle the variation in demand. There was a lot of variation. Relationship with the client leadership team. Credit worthiness. Risk levels. Size of loan. Date of the previous loan decision. Industry. Region. Each lending case was different. Yet the process treated them all the same. In particular the same sixty-two INFELS had to be prepared for each case. This took weeks and months.

We came up with an elegant way of giving clients a better and faster service by applying a 'what combination?' lens to the INFELS. The lending team had a quick meeting to review each lending application before it entered the process. Emphasis on before. There was a checklist of the sixty-two INFELS required. The team ran down the checklist and decided which combination of INFELS was needed for each application. This might be as few as eighteen INFELS for a regular client with repeating loans. This new approach gave a much-improved service to the client and significantly reduced the time and effort involved.

Cost and effort. This lens looks at the cost and effort of producing the INFEL. It may well be that the process does not need the INFEL at all. Perhaps it's a hangover from the past and no one has thought to challenge it. More frequent is where the INFEL is needed but can be produced at a fraction of the cost and effort. This case study is a carry on from the previous one and is a good example of this situation.

We applied the cost and effort lens to the sixty-two INFELS in the commercial lending process. How could we produce each INFEL with the least cost and effort – while maintaining quality.

One time and resource heavy INFEL was writing a report analysing the organisation applying for a loan. These reports were produced by internal analysts and would often run to fifty pages or more. One of the improvement team asked: 'Why are we writing these reports for well-known global companies when they are freely available from other sources?' We all looked at each other. Good point! The decision was made there and then. A faster way to produce the report INFEL at a fraction of the cost.

Timing. This lens looks at the timing of each INFEL. When is each INFEL used? Is it being used at the best possible time? Not too soon and not too late.

A hydropower generation company was optimising the use of their dams to ensure that they were getting the best prices for their electricity generation. A fifty-person team would work daily to define which of the dams on which of the rivers to run at which times based on multiple factors such as maintenance schedules, weather conditions and electricity prices.

We quickly established that time was of the essence. The more up to date the weather forecast or the more recent the latest coal prices, the better the optimisation. This was about mapping a large number of information elements together in order to understand how and when each bit of information was used as part of the optimisation. We took all of the INFELS and marked when this information was available and when it was used in the process. We then targeted the INFELS where there was a lag between when the data became available and when it was used. We were able to either use the information earlier or obtain the information later when it was more up to date – directly impacting both revenues and profits.

Predictability. This lens looks at the predictability of an INFEL's value.

A wind farm operator was experiencing problems in its 'Procure to Pay' process. Suppliers who were essential to their business were not getting paid on time because of issues with their invoices. The suppliers were subsequently holding back new supplies and this was causing severe operational problems. We did an INFELS analysis. There were over fifty INFELS in the process. Two of the most critical ones were budgeted cost and final cost. The process rejected invoices where the final cost was higher than budgeted cost. Hence the delays in paying suppliers.

Our analysis showed that the process had been designed on the basis that the INFELS were totally predictable. For example, a new computer notebook. I agree a price of one thousand euros with my supplier. That's the budgeted cost. If the invoice arrives with a cost of one thousand five hundred euros then the process should clearly reject it. But for some items the budgeted cost was highly unpredictable. Urgent repairs to an offshore wind turbine for example. There might be a storm so the repair ship or helicopter has to turn back and make a second trip. The actual cost could be double or treble the budgeted cost. The solution was to assign a predictability level to each type of procurement item and adjust the allowable margin of error between budgeted cost and final cost based on that predictability level.

These case studies demonstrate the power of INFELS analysis and the wide variety of lenses that you can apply. It's important to show your INFELS analysis in as visual and interesting a way as possible to colleagues involved. One way to do this is to show them as Post-it notes underneath your Value Stream Map. This is an elegant way to bring these two tools together.

Please see an example INFELS analysis in Figure 4.5. John is using the method to help get his dream job. While the process has just four steps, John has identified around thirty INFELS under these steps. Using a quality lens, he has realised that many of these INFELS are either below standard, such as his CV, or missing altogether, such as his social media presence. It's an urgent call to action to improve these INFELS in order to achieve his goals.

Mississippi Chart

The Mississippi Chart visualises the volume of demand flowing through the process. It is a fundamental tool of E2E improvements.

A good Mississippi Chart brings volumes alive. It shows how volumes and variations of work are flowing – or not flowing – through the organisation. Think of it as an X-ray machine. It takes an X-ray of the demand coming into the E2E process and what happens to it as it moves through the various steps, activities and

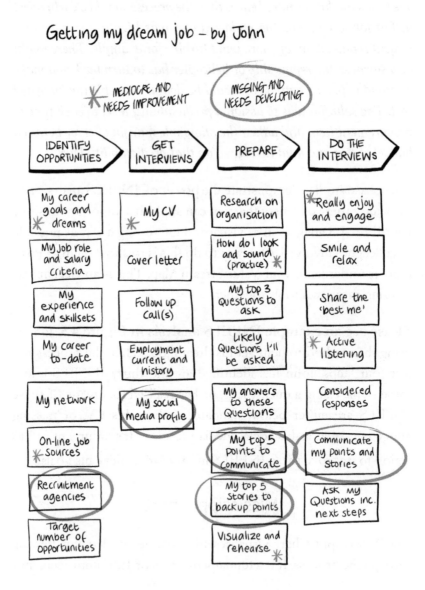

Figure 4.5 INFELS analysis example

teams. The Mississippi Chart is a highly visual tool. It makes it easy to see the failure demand, bottlenecks, defects, rework, issues and opportunities. All on one diagram.

The information from your Mississippi Chart can then be fed back into your Value Stream Map. These two tools support each other. Why is it called Mississippi Chart? *We were improving the E2E sales process of an outsourcing services company. We'd developed a new type of visual analysis to show how the work flowed through the organisation. There were endless loops and tributaries of rework. 'It looks like the Mississippi River, so many twists and turns!' exclaimed one of the participants. That was it. Our analysis tool had its name.*

1. How to create a Mississippi Chart

There are four steps to doing a Mississippi Chart.

1. **Define your hypothesis**

2. **Decide what to measure**

3. **Explore how the demand flows**

4. **Summarise issues, opportunities and performance**

1. Define your hypothesis. It is a good idea when doing a Mississippi Chart to define what you are looking for. This helps decide both what to measure and how to explore the demand flow. Otherwise it can grow arms and legs and not answer the right question. Having said that, you may find something completely different from what you expected. Which can be just as interesting and insightful. Here are five typical hypotheses:

• Process outcomes are not meeting customer purpose.

• There is significant failure demand.

- Lead and process times are too long and unpredictable.

- There is unnecessary cost and rework.

- There are severe capacity bottlenecks.

The hypothesis around value and failure demand can be so insightful that it deserves special consideration. Value demand is any demand going through the process that is providing value to the customer. Failure demand is handling failure in the process that is not providing value.

Emilia calls her bank to make a new loan request. This is value demand. Two weeks pass and Emilia has heard nothing. She calls her bank to ask what is happening to the loan request that she made two weeks ago. This is failure demand.

This demand is only happening because the E2E process is failing to provide what the customer wants. In this case, for progress to be fast and transparent so they don't have to waste time chasing things up. The concept of value demand and failure demand points the way to rapid improvement opportunities. Eliminate failure demand and handle value demand better.

Many of these hypotheses are connected. For example, failure demand by definition is not meeting customer purpose. It also triggers unnecessary cost and long unpredictable lead times. It is fine to test with more than one hypothesis.

2. Decide what to measure. The one metric that you always measure is volumes. Understanding volumes and how they flow through the various streams of your Mississippi is essential. Choosing the other metrics is a natural consequence of your hypotheses. For example, if your hypothesis is that there is unnecessary cost in the process then you measure the various costs at each stage of the demand flow. For capacity bottlenecks you would measure available capacity at each stage. For long lead times you would measure the lead time between stages.

I'd recommend measuring between three and five metrics at each stage of your Mississippi Chart. Typical ones include: volumes, process times, lead times, capacity available, costs and skills required.

3. Explore how the demand flows. A good place to start is with annual totals. The paths to explore can then be decided based on the hypotheses that you wish to explore. What's important is that the volume numbers that flow through the Mississippi chart are as meaningful and intuitive as possible.

There are three magic questions to explore and develop your Mississippi Chart. What happens next? What happens next? And what happens next? The Mississippi Chart will slowly come into focus. Keep asking and answering this question until you have a reasonable idea of how the demand is flowing through the organisation. Where are the delays? Where are the capacity issues? Where are the stockpiles of unfinished work? Where are the areas of rework? What are the frequent problems and where do they happen in the process? How long is each step taking? How much effort is required? And most important of all, how long is the whole E2E process taking?'

Most customers want a service or a product as soon as possible and with no problems, issues and delays. A typical reflection is: 'Why are we taking weeks and months to deliver a service riddled with errors and rework that we could deliver in hours and days if it flows smoothly and error free?'

4. Summarise issues, opportunities and performance. The Mississippi Chart is a visual tool. It makes it easy for people to see what the problem is and, just as important, where it is happening. Also how big a problem it is in terms of volumes. If the problem is happening to one per cent of the demand per year it may be a big problem but it will probably have a small impact. If it is happening to seventy per cent of the volume per year then it's probably having a big impact.

Mark up the hot spots, big issues and opportunities on your Mississippi Chart. Make it fun and interesting. Do whatever works visually to immediately draw the eye to the hot points and issues. For example, draw a pile of stones to represent queues and backlogs.

Finally, summarise the performance of your process and write this up on the Mississippi Chart. Typical measures are: right first time volumes that flow seamlessly through the process; total end-to-end lead time; total process times; total failure vs value demand and total people capacity. There are no hard and fast rules. Do whatever works.

Please see an illustration of a Mississippi Chart for mortgage applications in Figure 4.6. Notice how the chart highlights issues such as the waste caused by errors in application forms and opportunities such as the potential for cross-selling.

2. Hints and tips

Developing a Mississippi Chart is a learning experience. It is an art as well as a science. There is no one right way guaranteed to hit the jackpot every time. It's trial and error. Be prepared to go down a few blind alleys. Not a problem. You usually uncover some nuggets of gold on the way. Here are hints and tips to help your Mississippi Chart.

We don't know. Be prepared to say and to hear 'we don't know' to many of the questions that a Mississippi Chart prompts. Don't get discouraged. Just the opposite. Every time you hear or say a 'we don't know' think 'that's fantastic – we've highlighted a key gap in our knowledge. Let's go and find the answer.'

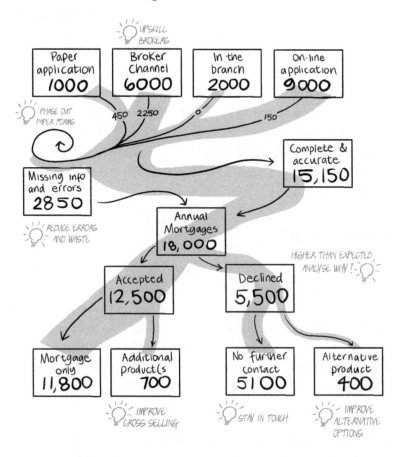

Mortgage Applications

Figure 4.6 Mississippi Chart example

Use estimates. When you don't know an answer I recommend writing estimates. Use red ink to highlight it's an estimate. This avoids blanks and highlights the numbers to go and find out. It keeps things moving and maintains positive momentum. It allows us to produce summary information at the end. Most important, it's an immediate call to action to go and find out the things we don't know.

Use ranges. Ranges are very useful when doing a Mississippi. There is often not an exact answer. Ranges allow us to be approximately right rather than precisely wrong. 'I'm not sure of the exact volume of applications that are filled out wrong but it's somewhere between thirty and forty per cent. Let's put that for now and make it an action to firm it up.'

3. Making it real

A good Mississippi Chart has a special ability to highlight problems and opportunities. Perhaps it's because the focus on volumes makes it so real for everyone. It's not a theoretical process map. It is volumes flowing through the process that everyone can relate to. And a Mississippi Chart is not just for E2E improvements. It can be equally helpful in TBT situations. This case study shows how a Mississippi Chart helped resolve long-standing friction and bad feeling between two teams.

The service desk and technical team at a telecommunications company had a frosty relationship. The issues had been occurring for years. A lot of frustration was created by lack of clarity over who was responsible for what work, how the work should be done and people 'closing' tasks incorrectly and 'taking credit'.

After understanding the symptoms, we created a Mississippi Chart by analysing a large quantity of task data to understand the flow of work between the two teams. This 'picture on a page' allowed us to have constructive conversations about facts and therefore prioritise the problems and dispel myths with the colleagues involved.

While creating the Mississippi Chart it became clear that the two departments had widely differing standard operating procedures and service level agreements. This was new information to both teams and greatly reduced the tension. A joint team was formed who worked side by side to focus on and fix the customers' issues including drafting a common set of operating procedures and measures.

Sharing what is happening

It's not enough to just find out what's happening today. We need to share and communicate it. Getting everyone involved on the same page in terms of the issues and opportunities is an essential backdrop to developing your new design. People must have the opportunity to ask questions, challenge and add their own builds and ideas. This is an essential part of the E2E improvement process. It dissolves silo-based thinking and builds the realisation that we're just a group of highly skilled and passionate human beings trying to make something better. This sharing experience is best done by getting everyone involved in the same location and running them through visuals of the SIPOC, Value Stream Map, INFELS analysis and Mississippi Chart. These normally fit as a group on a standard-sized wall. Between them they tell a comprehensive story of what is happening today.

This meeting is sometimes called a Report Out. We are reporting out everything we've learnt and giving everybody the chance to challenge, ask questions and make their own suggestions. The team of people from each area are reporting as a team to the leaders of each area. This may be a first. It gives enormous credibility to the message: 'This is what's happening at the moment' that it's coming from the people who are doing the work – as a team. Make it a stand-up meeting if possible. This makes it more informal and interactive. When someone makes a point or challenges a finding, write it on a Post-it note and stick it on the relevant location of the visuals.

This case study shows how a report-out session turned a pilot into a global deployment.

A consumer products company was rolling out 3D across its three largest regions. The Board had asked for an update on how it was going.

To make it interactive and keep PowerPoint to a minimum, we decided to run them through the Mississippi Chart that we had done for the 'Order to Cash' process for one of their leading brands in the USA. Our hypothesis was that a large number of orders were being touched by hand in what was supposed to be a fully automated process. Their goal was straight through processing. The Mississippi Chart had been done using Post-it notes on a six-foot by three-foot brown paper background. It had taken a one-day working session just asking: 'What happens next?' at each stage of the process. Often the answer was: 'We don't know' so we had then taken a week to get the detailed numbers behind each stage. To make it interesting, we turned it into a quiz where the actual numbers for each stage of the Mississippi Chart were covered up by Post-it notes with three multiple choice answers on each note. The Board members had to guess which number was right.

It was a bit of fun and only took thirty minutes. As we worked our way down the diagram it became clear that almost every order was touched by hand somewhere in the process. Only fifteen per cent of orders flowed through, right first time, and with no human intervention. The other eighty-five per cent had issues of one sort or another and needed manual intervention. This increased costs and delivery times, reduced customer satisfaction and delayed receipt of cash. The Board were aware that this core process – crucial to their strategic goals – had issues but not at this scale. The Mississippi Chart had visualised and communicated the scale, locations and impact of the problems with a new clarity. It created a wave of positive energy and support for the 3D initiative.

A few months later my role had finished and I was saying my farewells to the CIO who had sponsored the initiative. I asked him for his reflections. He replied, 'For me the most useful learning has been the power of the Mississippi Chart. Now when someone brings me an idea for a new system or technology project the first thing I ask is to see two Mississippi Charts. How the current demand is flowing through the system and how that demand is going to be better handled by the proposed new system. It gives us a new perspective on the benefits of technology initiatives.'

3. What is our vision for tomorrow?

There are two supplementary questions. **What are the principles underpinning our vision? And how will we measure success in achieving our vision?**

It is tempting at this point to rush into improving the process. 3D takes a slightly different approach. To pause and spend a short amount of time defining the vision for the process, the principles underpinning that vision and the measures for success in achieving the vision. To do this in advance of any new design work is a small investment with a big payback.

1. Vision

The vision reflects the customer's purpose in using the process. They are one and the same. The vision should be a succinct and inspiring way of expressing customer purpose. If we had to describe what we wanted our process to do in one – or two at most – sentences, what would we say? The key here is to keep it short and memorable. Less is more. Avoid a long convoluted sentence that no one can remember. 'We want to be the best of the best in the best possible way in all areas!' Meaningless No one remembers it.

I was at an event announcing the merger of two large organisations. The new leadership team, a combination from the previous two teams, had just come back from a one week off-site where they'd been developing the strategy and plan for the new organisation.

'We're really proud of our new vision' announced the CEO. He then tried to say it without a prompt card. It was about six lines long. 'Our vision is to be the best...' Halfway through he couldn't remember the wording. Embarrassed laughter. He turned to his number two: 'Sofia help me out here.' Sofia had a go. Unfortunately she couldn't remember it either! It was too long and convoluted. More embarrassed laughter. In the end, he brought up the vision PowerPoint slide and read it out. The audience was underwhelmed.

Defining the vision for your E2E process can be iterative. It does not have to be absolutely right first time. The important thing is to get to a first iteration and develop it from there. A first version should take thirty minutes to an hour. Get the improvement team together. Write the customer purpose on a flipchart so it's front of mind. Hand out Post-it notes and Sharpies. Tell the team members to spend ten minutes in silence writing down their idea or ideas for the vision statement. Then have each team member stick their one, two or three best ideas on a whiteboard and read them out loud. Next give the team six red dots each and tell them to vote on the statements they like best. No more than three dots on any one statement. Choose the most voted statement. Finally, see if there are any refinements to the most voted statement that will make it even better. Crisper. Sharper. More memorable. Go with this version as your first iteration. You can always improve it later.

We were improving our recruitment process. We decided on the following vision: 'Our vision is to recruit the right person in the right way in the right time.' Simple and easy to remember, it had a powerful impact on the new process. Here are just a few of the outcomes:

*- **The right person** triggered the development of new case studies and practical exercises to help really understand candidates skills and capabilities. Just as important to give candidates the best possible opportunity to demonstrate them. Imagine entering a singing contest and not being asked to sing!*

- The right way meant total respect for the candidate and making it an enjoyable experience. Total respect meant, amongst other things, rapid acknowledgement and feedback to the candidate at all times. No more waiting in a void wondering what's happening.

- The right time meant achieving end-to-end recruitment lead times that were a fraction of the previous times without compromising the process. In addition having the flexibility to fast track the process to a few days where the candidate had another job offer and needed to make a decision. A good example of having a standard way to handle variation.

2. Principles

This is the first supplementary question. What are the principles underpinning our vision? The principles are there to keep us honest in our new design. Principles are the guidelines for our design that help us create and evaluate potential solutions. If the solution is in line with our principles then it's in the mix. If it's out of line then we have a choice. We can either reject the solution or amend our principles. It is best to keep to between six to ten principles. Maybe twelve at a stretch. Any more and they become unwieldy.

To help bring the concept to life here are three design principles that I frequently recommend when I am part of an E2E improvement team.

• We trust our people to do a great job.

• We push decisions down to the lowest responsible and capable level.

• We have standard ways to handle variation.

Design principles like these can have a subtle and powerful influence. This is because no one can really object to them at the principles-setting stage. Of course we trust our people. Certainly, we want decisions made by the people on the ground with the most experience. Yes, if there's variation we need to handle it. Once accepted and agreed as principles, they support radical improvement ideas that might get rejected as stand-alone ideas later down the line.

1. We trust our people to do a great job. This is a really interesting principle. It is almost always gets accepted at this stage. No one wants to put their hand up and say: 'Actually, I propose that we don't trust our people to do a great job. Let's embed this distrust into our new design.'

And yet I've seen so many designs based on distrust of the people doing the work. Four eyes checks. Six eyes checks. Eight eyes checks. Approval after approval. The underlying assumption seems to be that if we build in enough approvals and checkpoints nothing will go wrong. It's not true. If everyone is responsible then no one is responsible. Much better to have the minimum responsible number of checks and approvals. And to have them at the lowest responsible and capable level. And in many cases this will be by the people doing the work.

Getting this principle accepted allows you to challenge a design solution that implies a lack of trust in the people doing the work. It's much harder to challenge these ideas without the backing of this principle. The conversation goes like this. Colleague: 'I recommend that we have three approvals here, here and here. This will ensure that nothing can ever go wrong.' You: 'Surely that's too many. It will slow down the process, take a lot more effort and doesn't show much faith in people doing the work.' Colleague: 'Are you recommending to add more risk to the process? Why would we do that?'

Compare this with the conversation when this principle has been agreed in advance. Colleague: 'I recommend that we have three approvals here, here and here. This will ensure that nothing can ever go wrong.' You: 'This idea goes against our principle to trust the people doing the work. If we really do trust them we don't need additional checks and approvals. They can approve their own work. Let's focus on excellent training so they have all the skills they need.'

This does not mean that we don't need approvals. Of course we do. But it's very easy and tempting to have more than necessary. Having this principle is a constant reminder to trust our people, make sure they receive the necessary skills and training to justify that trust and keep approvals down to the minimum responsible level.

2. We push decisions down to the lowest responsible and capable level. This is another powerful principle that is easy to agree to at the principles stage. It makes perfect sense. Why wouldn't we do this? But many – perhaps most – processes restrict decision making to the top levels. Many levels above the lowest responsible and capable level. This has negative implications on performance. It's disheartening for those doing the work that they are not trusted to make on-the-spot decisions. It causes bottlenecks. The senior people often aren't immediately available. Decisions and approvals stack up causing delays. It wastes large amount of leadership time doing work that is much better suited to the colleagues closer to the customer. It might seem that it is less risky. The thinking goes: surely if we keep all the decision making at the top then we are reducing the risks of something going wrong. In practice it's often the opposite. The people at the top are seldom in touch with what's really happening. I have a very personal example of how powerful it is to adopt this principle.

I had the privilege of building a team of 3D experts at Baringa. In the early days, I was involved in almost every decision. Recruitment, financial, operational, resourcing, planning, marketing and selling. Whatever the area, I was involved. When we were small this was okay. To be honest, it also made me feel important. Awareness of this ego dimension was a big learning for me.

As we grew, I became the bottleneck. I caused delay. I also caused stress in the team. People having to organise getting ten minutes of my time just to get a decision. And there were also decisions that I wasn't particularly good at. Juggling the resourcing of people on different projects is a good example. I can do it but I had teammates who were far better.

It couldn't go on! The team was fed up. I was fed up. So we went into a huddle and decided to adopt the principle to push every decision down to the lowest responsible level. We listed every type of decision that was made within the group. Sales decisions. Resourcing decisions. Recruitment decisions. Annual planning decisions. Operating decisions. Marketing decisions. We came up with a list of about forty decisions. This became a living document that we called our 'Decision Table'. We were ruthless in pushing down each decision to the lowest responsible level. We challenged ourselves on every decision. Could it go lower? Could we do additional training to enable it to go lower? Then we published and implemented our decision table. It worked so well we wondered why we'd taken so long. The benefits were immediate. Fewer delays and bottlenecks. Colleagues who felt empowered and responsible at every level. Less work for me. Most important of all, more informed decisions and better outcomes.

The Decision Table tool also provides real clarity on who is responsible for each decision. The key is to list out all the decisions at a granular level. Don't be vague. Be specific. This provokes the detailed discussion required for clarity.

It's also a call to action to build capability at the lowest responsible level. By deliberately moving away from the 'kick the decision upstairs' approach we shine a light on where we need to develop individual know-how and skills so that the person is qualified to make the decision.

3. We have standard ways to handle variation. This is another super powerful principle. People often take a little time to get their head around it. Then they love it! There are two types of variation: unnecessary and necessary. So a refinement on the above principle could be: 'We will remove unnecessary variation and have standard ways to handle necessary variation.'

Returning back to the earlier story about the global bank improving its commercial lending process. The crux of the problem was that the current process didn't really acknowledge or handle the variation in demand. What we needed was a standard way to handle this variation.

We came up with an elegant solution that I call the 'Deck of Cards'. Think of a deck of cards. If I asked you and a hundred other people reading this book to write down the names of all fifty-two playing cards, you'd all write down the same names. Excusing the odd error here and there. That's pretty impressive standardisation. Yet those same fifty-two cards can deliver near-infinite variation. Every time I deal ten cards they will be different.

The lending team decided 'which hand' to deal for each application. Just like dealing a hand from a pack of cards, this provided a standard way to handle the genuine variation involved in each lending decision.

3. Measures

This is linked to the second supplementary question: **How will we measure success in achieving our vision?** Remember that our vision reflects the customer's purpose in using the process. Therefore our measures should also be based on customer purpose. Aligning measures with vision and purpose is the key to success. How we are measured – or how we measure ourselves – drives our behaviours. If I'm measured on achieving the vision then I'll strive to make that happen. So will my colleagues. We are aligned behind a common purpose. The customer's purpose.

This can be an incredibly quick win in E2E process improvement. The quickest win and least cost solution is to stop doing something! It has immediate impact and it saves money. We often find in our E2E improvement work that people and teams are being measured on internal targets that have little or nothing to do with customer purpose. This causes people to – quite naturally – act in ways that are perfectly sensible for their personal survival and well-being but act directly against achieving the vision and customer purpose. What's the solution? Use measures that reflect the vision and customer purpose and, whenever possible, remove those that don't.

4: What is the new design to achieve our vision?

Creating our new design can be surprisingly straightforward. It is a natural outcome of the foundation work in the E2E Checklist Questions One, Two and Three. Combine this foundation work with our vision, principles and measures, and the design can become obvious. It often seems to fall out of our previous work.

This section covers four tools to help create the new design. They each provide a different perspective. The four tools are:

- **The Really Device**

- **Crazy Eight Brainstorming**

- **Eliminate, Combine, Rearrange, Simplify, Standardise (ECRSS)**

- **Universal Solutions**

Use them in this order. Start with the Really Device. Why? Because it provides the link to our earlier work and ensures we lock onto a design that fulfils vision and customer purpose. At this point, the design will be high level. Then do a Crazy Eight Brainstorm. Why? Because it gets everyone's ideas on the table before detailed solutions are selected. It drives optionality. It ensures we don't jump to a solution while not even considering a better option. Then use ECRSS to develop the detailed design. Finally use Universal Solutions as a sweep up to make sure no opportunities are missed.

Using these four tools and the different perspectives they provide is relatively easy and quick. The whole exercise can usually be done in a couple of working sessions. They work together to get creative juices flowing and the team's best ideas on the table. This section finishes with a case study: **Bringing it all together** where this four-way approach generated a breakthrough process design.

The Really Device

The Really Device inserts the word 'really' into three customer design questions.

- What do our customers **really** want?

- What **really** matters to our customers?

- How do we design around what our customers **really** wants and what **really** matters?

The power of these three questions lies in their simplicity. They ensure we stay one hundred per cent focused on the customer and the customer's purpose in using the process. Note that each question includes the word customer. Also that we keep the design at a high level. We can go into the details later. The **really** questions help us avoid three common traps during the design stage. Improving something that we shouldn't be doing at all. Creating a design that ignores the issues. Missing transformational opportunities.

This last point is important. Answering the three **really** questions encourages transformational thinking. It gives us an outside-in view. 'Forget what we are doing at the moment. What should we be doing?' It avoids the traditional inside-out view: 'This is what we've always done. How can we do it a bit better?' We'll see an example of this transformational thinking and design in the case study for this tool.

We know the answers to **really** questions one and two from our earlier E2E work. They provide the essential link to this work. They ensure that our new design takes full advantage of these learnings. Let's focus on **really** question three: How do we design around what the customer **really** wants and what **really** matters?

3D takes a holistic approach. Our answer to this question needs to consider all possible factors. Measures, process activities, information elements, skills and capabilities, technology, organisation structure. Plus one special factor: leadership thinking. Specifically: 'What was the leadership thinking that resulted in the current state? And does this leadership thinking need to change to sustain our new design?'

The Government had mandated that every home and business in the country must have a smart meter installed for energy usage. We were helping a client roll out these new meters to its millions of customers within government deadlines. It was a race against time and the race was too tight for comfort.

The current process was that when a customer phoned in to request a new smart meter they would be given a time slot in three weeks time for an appointment with an engineer. Customers would often call to rearrange the appointment, or worse, the engineer would arrive to an empty property as the customer had forgotten to be at home. This triggered long delays, additional cost, unhappy customers and frustrated engineers.

The improvement team started to dig into reasons behind the three weeks policy. Why was this the case? Nobody knew, they just followed the rules. They had to because they were regularly assessed by the quality assurance team and it would impact their bonus if they deviated from the script. The team finally identified that it was the planning and dispatch team who needed to keep their engineers busy. Having three weeks allowed them to optimise their teams and drive productivity. But it wasn't really working. Yes, people were being kept busy but often on non-productive, wasteful activities such as arriving at empty homes.

The current process was designed from an internal perspective. We used the Really Device to redesign it from the customer's perspective.

- *What does our customer really want? To get their smart meter installed as soon as possible once they've requested one. And at a time that suits them and they know they will be in.*

- *What really matters to our customer? Getting it right first time. Fast easy process. Short time between request to install. No rescheduling or delays.*

- *How do we design around what the customer really wants and what really matters? Ask the customer when they would like the meter installed including the option of next day installation. Most customers know where they will be the next day.*

The leadership team were innovative. Although cautious about the feasibility of this approach they agreed to run a test in one part of the country to see what would happen. The outcome exceeded all expectations. Failed appointments dropped by seventy per cent. The Net Promoter Score (NPS) for the teams involved in the test shot up. The cost savings were measured in the tens of millions.

Crazy Eight Brainstorming

Crazy Eight Brainstorming gets its name from taking a piece of A4 paper and folding it three times. This produces eight areas on the A4 bordered by the fold lines. Participants then have one minute to draw or write an improvement idea in the first area. After the first minute, the facilitator calls out 'move to number two' and, whether finished or not, each team member then draws or writes a second improvement idea in the second area. This goes on for eight minutes by which time each team member will have generated eight improvement ideas. Participants then share and prioritise their ideas. The whole exercise takes about an hour.

Participants are usually surprised how well it works and at the number and quality of great ideas that come out of an eight-minute exercise. There are several reasons why the Crazy Eight is so effective.

Gets the brain cells fizzing! Doing a Crazy Eight has a curious impact on the brain. You need to do it to experience it. By the time you get to idea five or six your brain is getting squeezed. Your thought patterns go into a different place. Your neurons are firing on all cylinders. You start to come up with innovative and original ideas. I'm not a brain expert so I'm not going to pretend I understand it. I just know that it happens. I've facilitated many Crazy Eights and the feedback is usually: 'Wow, that was amazing. I can't believe we generated so many great ideas in such a short time.'

Creates a safe environment. It means that no idea is silly or too wild and wacky. That's the point. It breaks down the caution and conservative boundaries that can all too easily limit our thinking. It makes it safe to throw out an idea that might get shot down in a more everyday work environment. We've all been in meetings where someone's said something a bit off the wall and there's a deafening silence, a few people roll their eyes and the facilitator says: 'Thank you Pat. Shall we move on?' Pat feels terrible and everyone else dries up. The Crazy Eight makes it safe to share your wildest and most innovative ideas.

Gets everyone's ideas out. Each person has a quiet period to go into their own head space and generate their individual ideas ahead of any group discussion. This ensures that everyone's ideas get on the table. Sometimes the best idea comes from the quietest person. It's all too easy for one or two people to dominate an open brainstorming session. The more introverted team members may say nothing. Then, like little kids chasing a football, we have a tendency to chase after the first idea that someone suggests. This burns up valuable time. Some brilliant ideas may never be heard.

Supports good communication. The exercise provides a robust framework for high-value group discussion. No one dominates. No one feels left out. Each person has the opportunity to share and describe their ideas to the group without interruption – except for clarification questions.

A Middle Eastern oil company had well-established marketing and retailing operations in place. These covered both national and international markets. It wanted to move into trading oil and associated products as well as marketing and retailing. Trading would require a whole new technology, processes and governance infrastructure. It was a multi-year programme costing tens of millions of dollars.

We were teaching the 3D framework and running the Crazy Eight exercise as part of the course. One of the colleagues had the 'crazy' idea to just start trading. He explained his Post-it note to his colleagues. 'We could just start with a very minor low-risk low-volume product. We don't need to wait for the heavyweight technology. We could manage with what we already have plus some lightweight add-ons. The advantage is that this will start to build our culture and skills in trading. There will be lots of learnings for the bigger programme and we can minimise the risks with a simple governance structure.'

The team got excited and fleshed out the idea in more detail. What were the risks? How could they be mitigated? What training was required? Who would be on the test team? What were the benefits? When could they start? The next day there was a report out to the senior leadership team. The CEO listened in silence and then said: 'I have one question and one comment.' My question is: 'What are the risks and how will you handle them? My comment is that provided the risks are well managed then please proceed as soon as possible. This will give us the learnings and experience that we need ahead of – not after – the implementation of our new trading system. Please develop the plan.' The team was amazed by the speed and positivity of the leadership response to an idea created in eight minutes.

Eliminate, Combine, Re-arrange, Simplify, Standardise

Eliminate, Combine, Rearrange, Simplify, Standardise is often abbreviated to ECRSS. It asks five questions in a particular order. We already have a high-level new design from the Really Device and Crazy Eight Brainstorming. These five questions help us develop the details of our design. Let's look at each question in turn.

1. Eliminate. What can we just stop doing? Number one on the list is waste. Eliminate the waste. Refer to section: **Grounded in Lean thinking** for a list of wastes to look for and eliminate. Think big. Keep a wide scope. It's not just activities and process steps that add no value to the customer. Measures that drive the wrong behaviour. Reports that no one reads. Confusing and out-dated policies. Over-engineered governance and approvals. Actions that are causing self-inflicted unnecessary variation. It's all in scope!

This is a powerful question because it provides immediate quick wins at zero cost. In fact, less than zero cost. Stopping doing things costs less not more. And the impact is immediate. It's the first question because there's no point improving or rearranging or simplifying something that we shouldn't be doing at all.

2. Combine. Now that we've eliminated as much non-value-add work as possible, it's time to combine. What activities can we bring together so that there are no hand-offs and delays? Remember that hand-offs are always a potential weak link in the chain. Hand-offs cause delays. Piles of inventory and work-in-progress. Queues. Defects and errors. Capacity imbalances. As you can tell I'm not a huge fan of hand-offs. Sometimes I'll look at a Value Stream Map of twenty-two steps and think: 'No wonder this process is so broken. How can it be streamlined with twenty-two steps? It can't!' One question I always ask: 'Why do we need any steps at all? Why can't it all be done in one step?' This is typically not possible but it's a great challenge to put to the team.

3. Rearrange. Let's recap. We've removed any steps and activities that we don't need to do. That don't add value to the customer. And are not necessary for internal purposes. And then we've combined as many activities as possible to remove hand-offs. The next step is: 'What can we rearrange? Are we doing things in the best order?' The answer is often no. Innovative restaurant chains are good examples of the amazing results that can be achieved simply by rearranging things. Here's a couple of examples.

- A gourmet burger restaurant rearranges 'order-eat-pay' to 'order-pay-eat'. It takes payment up front at the time of ordering. I'm having a quick lunch with a colleague. Benefit? No waiting for the bill (and the many iterations that always seem to be involved.) Now we can just get up and leave as soon as we are finished.

- A Japanese fast food restaurant rearranges 'order your food-see your food' to 'see your food-order (take) your food. They use a conveyor belt to continuously move bowls of different items in front of me. Benefits: No delay between ordering and eating. Real-time feedback to the chefs on what to cook next. Just look for the missing bowls. Eating several items that I hadn't planned to because they look so delicious. (Not sure that's a benefit!)

4. Simplify. We've eliminated the waste. Combined remaining activities to remove hand-offs. Rearranged them into the best order to meet customer purpose. Now – and only now – it's time to simplify. Notice the logic of the order of ECRSS. It avoids simplifying something that we may end up eliminating altogether. Or simplifying an activity that ends up being combined with another activity.

Think big and bold in terms of simplification. Keep every element in scope. It's not just activities. Policies, approvals, roles, responsibilities, forms, user guides, calculations, process steps, organisation design and IT system screens. They can all be simplified. And it's usually a quick win. Doing less not more for the same or better result. And doing less usually costs less.

5. Standardise. Let's recap yet again on the order of the ECRSS method. It has a relentless logic. First we eliminated non-value activities. Then we combined the value-add activities to reduce hand-offs. Next we rearranged the combined activities into the most effective order. Only then did we simplify them as much as possible. Finally – and only now – is the right time to standardise. This sequence ensures that we avoid, for example, standardising an over-complicated activity; or standardising a non-value-add process that should be eliminated.

Standardising is the ultimate in common sense. It means agreeing the current best way to meet customer purpose and then mandating that everyone follows this best way. There are some understandable challenges to standardising. For one thing it can sound a bit boring. I often hear comments like: 'I'm creative! I like to do things in my own way.' Or 'I know a better way to do this job than the standard way that we all have to follow. So I'm going to do it my way.' I think this is a valid view if standardisation is done in the wrong way. There are three nuances that need to be added to standardisation. First the standard way should be communicated as the current best way. That's what it is: 'The current best way.' What it's not is: 'The standard way that can't ever be changed even if it's clearly not the best way!' Second, and this is closely linked to the first, it's the foundation for continuous improvement. It's today's foundation for something better tomorrow. So paradoxically, standardisation supports creativity. Thirdly it's a half-truth. We don't just want standard ways. We want more. We want a standard way to handle the variation. This idea is expanded in section: **E2E Q2: What is happening today?**

Universal solutions

There are a number of solutions that have universal application to process improvement. This section provides a high-level overview of seven of these universal solutions:

1. **Quality at Source**

2. **Error Proofing**

3. **Single Piece Flow**

4. **Capacity Balancing**

5. **Visual Management**

6. **Cell Pod Working**

7. **Five S**

I like to use restaurant examples to bring these solutions to life in a way that is easy to relate to.

1. Quality at Source. My favourite universal solution. Simple. Common sense. Immediate impact. The quality at source of its ingredients is the first priority of any restaurant. It doesn't matter how talented the chef is; how beautiful the decor and the lighting; how helpful and attentive the staff. If the meat is off and the vegetables are mouldy – forget it. It's over. Unhappy customers, reputational damage, word spreads and no one returns. It's the same with processes. Once you get bad parts or data into the process, they're hard to get out. I use the analogy of pouring sugar into a car's petrol tank. It only takes a few seconds but once it's in the engine it's impossible to get out. A horrible thought. The car is a write-off. It's the same with processes. Often the process grinds on until right at the end when the product or service is rejected. The process has to start again with unhappy customers, wasted cost and effort, and long and unpredictable lead times. The answer is quality at source. Treat your source data and parts like food ingredients in a top-class restaurant!

The further a product or a response to a request flows down a process the more value it accrues because we have spent more time and resources on it.

Matt was in charge of the turbine blade casting team of a renowned aircraft engine manufacturer. Every component starts life as a wax version of the end product. Any defects in the wax version will result in a very expensive scrap metal casting later on. So when there was a big push to improve process yields, Matt and his team focused all their energy on perfecting the wax inputs. The tooling was refreshed and the team were retrained and reminded of their criticality. Because all the money is made at the 'cheap' end of the process.

2. Error Proofing. A first cousin to quality at source. Error proofing is as it sounds. How can we avoid making errors and get it right first time? It applies to every type of work. Manufacturing and service. It's often a low cost solution that punches far above its weight. There are basically three levels of error proofing - going from strongest to weakest.

- Prevent an error. This is the strongest level. Designing the product or process or service so that it is impossible to make an error. *A good example is the design of SIM card for your mobile phone. Notice how the cut off corner on the card and the matching shape on your phone makes it impossible to put in the wrong way round.*

Here's another example which proves the point. Almost. *The design of a USB stick is frequently used as a good example of error proofing. The assumption is that it's impossible to put in the wrong way around. When my daughter was five years old she proved that it's actually reasonably easy to put in the wrong way around. You just have to push hard enough! She used my notebook computer which had three USB ports to test her hypothesis and in ten minutes all three ports were broken. Thanks Lucy!*

A common variation on preventing an error is to make it less likely. There are many instances where we can't guarantee prevention but we can greatly reduce the probability. Simply by using our creative juices and usually at little or no cost. Designing forms is a classic case. Both paper based and on-line. Most information is transmitted via forms. Bad form design triggers large amounts of waste. The solution is simple: Use the excellent information readily available on good form design. As a taster, here is the first of thirteen best practice principles from CXL.com. *Less is more (i.e. remove form fields): Every field you ask users to fill out increases friction. The best thing you can do to improve form completions is to get rid of as many fields as possible. In one case study, an 11-field contact form was replaced with a 4-field version, and form completions increased by 160%. (The quality of submissions stayed the same.)* (Birkett, A. 2019)[1] We often think of errors in terms of mistakes. This principle expands on that. It is classifying failure to complete the form as an error. Perhaps the most expensive error of all.

- Raise an alarm as soon as an error is made. This is the next level of error proofing. The alarm can be a noise or a light or a visual sign. Anything that raises immediate awareness. The point is to catch and rectify the error as soon as it is made and stop it flowing on down the process often triggering exponential increases in costs and waste. It can also act as an immediate call to action to find the root cause. And it's easier to find the root cause if the error is spotted at source. Let's look at a couple of examples: *Manufacturing production lines use flashing lights and/or sirens to alerts operators when a defect is identified. The line is often stopped until the problem is fixed. This stops the error flowing downstream and creates urgency to fix the problem and find the root cause.*

A web form is designed so that the user gets immediate feedback when they make a mistake. For example typing in a mobile phone number with too few numbers. The error message is clear and in friendly language such as: 'Whoops, too few numbers, please try again.' Not: 'Error Code 4386!'

- Check to see if an error has been made. This is the third and weakest form of error control. It should be the last choice. Too often it's the first because it's the easy option. Frequently heard comments: 'Let's put additional approvals in here and here.' 'Let's set up a quality control team to check the final product.' No actually let's not! Let's be creative and think of ways to ensure that defects and errors can't happen in the first place.

3. Single Piece Flow. Single piece flow is as the name suggests. It is an approach where the product or service is made and delivered as a single piece. Not in batches. So it keeps moving. This keeps it flowing as fast and smoothly as possible to the end customer. It also helps remove the waste that can often hide unnoticed when things are made and delivered in batches. Single piece flow works hand-in-hand with the concept of pull. This is where the signal to make a product or deliver a service is triggered by actual customer demand. The product is pulled by customer demand. It's not pushed by productivity targets. This avoids the waste of over-production. And the accompanying wastes of defects, delays and transport that go with over-production.

A fast-growing chain of Mexican food restaurants uses single piece flow and pull to create a brilliant customer experience. How does it work? My three friends and I sit at the table. Our server gives each of us a large A3-sized disposable paper menu and a crayon. I draw a circle around each item I want. We are pulling our order. Nothing is made until we pull. No one in the kitchen is pushing out burritos in the hope that they'll be wanted. Or to meet their personal burritos target!

The server tells us that each item will come as soon as it's ready. This is single piece flow in action. I get my chicken taco before Reena gets her vegetable burrito because my meal is ready first. Unlike other restaurants, our meal is not being batched up until all four meals are ready. My chicken taco is fresh and hot. Not lukewarm and stale while my friends' meals are cooked. The ingredients are always fresh and delicious by the way. Quality at source!

Here's another case study where using single piece flow transformed the outcome for all concerned.

A home appliance repair company was streamlining their repairs scheduling process. This involved visiting customer homes to repair their home appliances such as washing machines and dryers. The current process was that the customer would call in and request the repair and the company would call them back a few days later with the appointment time. The problem was the long lead times between the customer request, the company call back and the engineer's attendance date. In practice, it was often two weeks or more from request to appointment. This triggered its own problems in terms of customers not being in on the scheduled date, forgetting they'd requested the update and even changing their mind. It was all too difficult and clunky!

As part of our analysis we discovered that the customer service team was consolidating the appliance repair requests through the week and then releasing them in one batch to the scheduling team each Friday. Meanwhile the scheduling team developed and released their weekly schedule to the field engineers each Thursday. This meant that a customer calling in with a fault on a Monday would not even be scheduled for an engineer's visit for ten days! It turned out that two years earlier the head of scheduling – long since gone – had requested getting all the requests in one go as it 'made scheduling easier'.

The answer was obvious. We implemented single piece flow for each customer request. No batching. No delays. Now when a customer requested an appliance repair the request flowed straight through to the scheduler in minutes. Using the latest information including real-time engineer locations and daily schedule completion rates, they would often book the visit for the same or next day.

Replacing batch with single piece flow achieved happier customers, lower costs, and less stress and rework for the teams involved.

4. Visual Management. As previously mentioned, visual management can be summed up by the saying: 'See together, know together, act together.' Let's look at each in turn.

- See together: We can see across the E2E process what is happening now – in the present. What has happened in the recent past. And what is expected from us personally.

- Know together: We know our goals, when things are on track, going wrong or about to go wrong if we don't take remedial action very quickly.

- Act together: This is where the rubber hits the road. We do much more than just see and know. We act together as a team to make the plan happen. If things are on track, that's great. If things are going awry, we take remedial action.

A car dealership and service company was not meeting customer expectations for reliable and predictable service times. Customers would often be called at the last minute to say their car was not ready for collection. Could they come the following day? Sometimes they were already on their way. This was hitting its reputation, customer base, service and sales revenues.

The improvement team explored what was happening. The main cause was that it was often early afternoon before the service desk realised that they were running late. The problem was fixed with a simple visual management solution. The team designed a filing system where each job for the day went into its own folder. The folder went into a wooden storage unit with vertical slots for each thirty-minute period of the working day. So the slot marked 930–1000 might have three folders in it. This meant that these three jobs were due to start during that period. If by 1030 there were still folders in the 930–1000 slot it was an early warning that the days schedule was slipping behind. Additional resources could be allocated to the work or the customer could get an early warning.

The visual management device also improved the working culture. Everyone in the service bays watched it constantly. Everyone knew the implications and supported each other to achieve the day's schedule. **Please see an illustration of this device in Figure 4.7.** It's 12.30pm and the visual display has just triggered a remedial action to get things back on track.

5. Capacity Balancing. We looked at capacity balancing and cross-skilling in TBT ways of working. They are equally powerful solutions in an E2E context. Every E2E process will have a series of activities in sequential or parallel flow or both. It only takes one of those activities to have a capacity problem to impact the whole process. Not just the activity with the capacity problem. In this sense there is an amplified benefit of good capacity balancing across all activities in the process.

The reality is that capacity balancing is a continual improvement. It's not a one-and-done. It's a continual challenge. Demand peaks and troughs, changing demand patterns, people changes, skills changes. They all impact capacity peaks and troughs.

An engine parts manufacturing facility flexed its resource as a standard way of working. Colleagues were cross-skilled to do different activities and roles through the week as the work moved through

Figure 4.7 Visual Management example

the process. This ensured productivity, provided job variation and created agility in the workforce if the customer demand plan changed and issues incurred. The available capacity was continually balanced across the work to be done.

Here is another example that many of us will have seen in action.

One of the world's most successful gourmet fast food outlets makes an art out of capacity balancing and cross training. All their food is prepared on-site. The E2E process turns raw ingredients into a variety of delicious soups, sandwiches, baguettes, sushi, fruit drinks and hot beverages. The staff are cross-skilled in the wide range of skills required to make this happen. Preparing the food. Making coffees and teas. Serving customers. Restocking the shelves based on what has sold. Pull in action.

The staff are continually capacity balancing across the processes involved. Most staff are preparing food during the early morning quiet period. More switch to service during the eight-to-nine breakfast peak period. And so the capacity balancing dance goes on through the day, continually adjusting to demand volumes and variations. Notice how essential cross-skilling and up-skilling are to making this work. If only one person could make cappuccinos there would soon be queues, delays and unhappy customers!

6. Cell Pod Working. This is a powerful way of organising work that combines many of the benefits of the other universal solutions and ECRSS. For this reason, it deserves special attention. It is frequently the key to transformational change. The concept is simple. Bring everyone involved in the E2E process together into a single team. The various activities required to make one unit of a product or service are carried out by one team located in the same physical or virtual area. There are numerous advantages. It enables a single unit to flow smoothly across all the activities with no delays or batching. It brings people to the work. There is joint accountability for everyone in the

171

cell pod. The cell pod can adopt a single set of measures based on customer purpose. It supports visual management. It shines a light on up-skilling and cross-skilling opportunities. Capacity balancing in the cell pod can be real-time based on actual demand.

A utilities company traditionally worked their processes in a functional model where work passed from Function A to Function B to Function C to complete the processes. There were often five or more functions involved in a process. This resulted in silos in the organisation, quality issues and large lead times to process work. We worked with them to implement a cellular pod structure. They brought together resources from each function into multi skilled teams that managed each end-to-end process within a single team.

The benefits were immediate and profound. Lead times reduced to the process time that it took to do the work as there were no hand-offs. Individual skills and capabilities grew as colleagues learnt from each other and rotated activities. Defects and mistakes reduced and were fixed on the spot. Best of all, the cellular pod empowered the colleagues and created end-to-end accountability for the customers' outcomes as the work had nowhere else to go.

You can see an illustration of a Cell Pod team in Figure 4.8. What special characteristics do you notice compared to a single function team?

7. Five S. The five Ss stands for Sort, Set (in order), Shine, Standardise and Sustain. In many work environments it is a way of life. Especially in manufacturing. Some improvement initiatives make Five S the foundation of their approach. Let's quickly run through each S in turn. Then we'll look at examples to make the concept come alive.

1. Sort: Only keep what you need to do the work. Throw away or remove the rest.

Figure 4.8 Cell Pod in action

2. Set (in order): Remember the saying: 'A place for everything and everything in its place.' That's what Set is. Our clutter has been drastically reduced. Now we organise what remains.

3. Shine: This means more than simply to shine. It means to maintain and keep in perfect working order as well as to keep clean.

4. Standardise: The next step is to look at every item and ask, 'Where and how can we standardise our materials, equipment and physical layouts?' In this context, Standardise also means optimise.

5. Sustain: The fifth and final stage. Implementing daily working practices to ensure our new environment is sustained. There's no point in doing the first four Ss if it all reverts to an untidy mess in a few days or weeks.

A global fast food organisation, famous for its burgers, runs its restaurants on strict Five S principles. Everything is spotless. Every piece of equipment has its own storage place, is immediately to hand and has been optimised for its role. The French fries scoop is an example. It has been designed to perfection to deliver the exact amount of fries with the minimum hand and arm motion. There are procedures for every tiny operating detail. All staff are fully trained and familiar with these procedures. This mandatory way of working and its impact on the food, customer experience and operating efficiency is one reason why this organisation grew to be a global giant in just ten years.

Five S is not new. It's been a way of life at sea for hundreds of years. The principles behind Five S are paramount to the safety of a ship and her crew. *A sailing boat is an excellent example of Five S as an embedded culture. There is a place for everything and everything in its place. The decks are scrubbed clean. Every rope is neatly coiled. There are foam cut-outs for vital tools. If a tool is missing you can spot it immediately. There are regular checks on every piece of equipment. If something breaks it is repaired or replaced immediately. The cabins and cooking galleys are spotless. There is no clutter. No unnecessary items. And every necessary item has its own place. And a safe place. If a storm blows up, the equipment is safe and secure.*

Five S is about much more than decluttering, organising and cleaning the workplace. It is about effectiveness, health and safety. A Five S environment is a foundation support for effective performance and safety. It is also a lot nicer to work in. Most of us just feel better working in a Five S environment.

These universal solutions have universal applicability. Not just at work but also at home.

Anu had been doing process improvement and workplace transformation for clients for many years. It was only after she had kids that she realised how much these skills could help her get some sanity in her life at home. The mornings were a massive stress! She calculated that it took her and her husband about an hour and a half to get their two kids, both under five, ready and out of the door every morning, invariably just rushing in as the school gates closed.

This wasn't sustainable. She decided to apply all her skills and learnings at home. Anu's root cause analysis showed that instead of constructive activities, she spent most of her time negotiating and bargaining on clothes and breakfast. This led to repetition, errors and delays. Once she had the root cause, it didn't take long to reorganise the cupboards to get everything in one place which a five-year-old could reach. Adding visual reminders worked like a charm in making sure her kids could dress themselves properly for the day ahead.

You can see an illustration of Anu's kids' bedroom in Figure 4.9. How many Universal Solutions can you see working together?

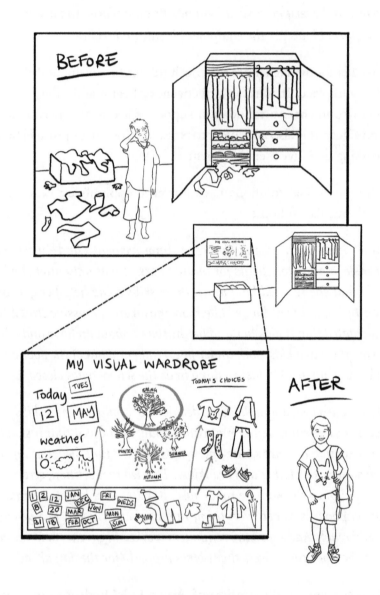

Figure 4.9 Visual Management at home

Helpful design tips

Here are a couple of tips that I personally always use at the design stage. They may seem a bit unusual but they work.

1. Meditate. That's not a typo. Meditate by yourself for thirty minutes or so. There is normally a team room where all the current state analysis work is up on the walls. The SIPOC, VSM with INFELS and Mississippi Chart. It's a visual space. I wait until everyone has gone to lunch or left for the day and I go into the room by myself. And I just look at the visual displays. And pretend to be the customer. And focus on what I **really** want and what **really** matters. What would I love to happen? Not like to happen but love to happen. After fifteen or twenty minutes of silence the visuals start talking to me. And the new design starts to fall out of the displays.

2. First draft with small core group. Get together with a small core group from the improvement team. Usually around two to three colleagues. Go into the team room and brainstorm a first draft of the design. Then use this design as the straw man for the first design meeting with the wider team.

This might seem a bit odd. Doesn't it lack inclusivity? But I've found it works better than starting off with the whole team and a blank sheet of paper. It enables radical transformational ideas to be put on the table – semi-formed – that might never get off the ground with the whole team in the room. It's faster. The wider team often prefers a draft idea to build and improve on rather than a blank sheet of paper.

Bringing it all together

This case study shows how the four design tools were used in sequence to create a breakthrough new design.

A legal insurance organisation wanted to improve their end-to-end sales process. This is when a small- or medium-sized business needs to take out legal insurance for their business. The insurance covers the legal costs of defending a lawsuit against the business.

We analysed what was happening today. The customer purpose was a surprise. Customers were busy trying to grow their business. Most saw taking out legal insurance as a necessary but low priority action. They wanted to get it done in minutes. With the minimum fuss and paperwork. Customers wanted a basic, easy to understand, low-cost product. Yet the current situation was exactly the opposite! Customers spent hours and multiple calls trying to get through to the right person to talk to. The sales team were all lawyers. They had to have the necessary expertise. They had individual assistants who did their typing and they sat in their own offices behind closed doors.

A team of telephone receptionists handled the incoming calls. They then routed the calls to whichever assistant was available. Most of the time the sales lawyers were busy so the assistants took a note of the customer details and said someone would call them back. There were no time standards. The sales lawyer would call back the same day, the next day or even the day after, depending on their workload. When the customer did, at last, speak with a sales lawyer, it was often the wrong sales lawyer for their industry and the whole process would start again. It could take several days for the customer to just start talking to the right person. Let alone buy the product. It was taking an average of nine days to do two hours work!

Customer feedback on the insurance products was mixed. Smaller businesses saw them as too complex, expensive and difficult to understand. In an effort to satisfy the most demanding customers, the product development team had designed a range of products that were gilt-edged and over-engineered. Most customers wanted something basic, low cost, easy to understand and quick to buy. They were offered something very different. The conversion rate of enquiries to sales was less than twenty-five per cent. The client was losing market share and reputation.

*We started with the **Really** device. What do our customers **really** want? To buy a solid legal insurance product from a trusted provider and get it off their to-do list. What **really** matters to our customers? Cost-effective, trusted insurer and minimal time and effort. How do we design around **really** wants and **really** matters? I used my personal meditation technique and went into the project room by myself during a lunch break. I stared at the value stream map. About ten feet long and sixteen activity blocks of hand-offs, rework and waste. And time. Lots of time. Especially customer time! When the team got back from lunch I organised a working session with two colleagues and outlined my idea. 'It's all about time. These business owners are really busy. This is bottom of their list of priorities. They just need to get it done as quickly as possible. How can we make that happen?'*

We organised a Crazy Eight session in the afternoon. In square seven I wrote down: 'The first person you talk to is the last person you talk to.' Hmmm, what did that mean. I pretend to be a customer and ask myself what I'd love to happen. Suddenly it's obvious. I'm at my desk. Looking at my to-do list. OK, time to get legal insurance knocked off the list. I call the legal insurance sales number and get straight through on the second ring. 'Hi I'm Lucia, how can I help you?' 'Hi Lucia, I'm James. I own a small sports equipment retailer in the centre of town and I'm looking to get my legal insurance. Can I speak to someone who can help me?' 'Hi James. That's me. I'm a lawyer and can help you on this. And I'll be your contact from now on. Can I ask you a few questions...?' A few minutes later... 'OK James that's fine. I'll email you the pre-completed form for your signature and return. You can sign it electronically if that's easiest. This will also have my email and direct contact number. Please just email or call me direct if you have any questions or points to discuss.' 'Thanks Lucia. That's great.'

This is exactly what happened. The entire business was transformed. Four regional centres replaced twenty-two local offices. The receptionist and administration teams moved to other roles. The communications network was upgraded. Sales lawyers moved out of their offices into a circular open plan layout with large visual displays showing who was managing which cases. The sales lawyers were up-skilled and cross-skilled to handle a wider variety of cases. A new line of simple and fast products was developed and launched. The marketing message was changed to: 'Protecting your business and your time!'

This is an extreme example. Not every E2E improvement leads to transformation on this scale. But it's exciting when it does!

5: How can we test and deploy our new design with agility?

It is well known that improvement initiatives often fail at the point of implementation. Study after study show failure rates of anywhere from fifty to seventy per cent. Everything is going swimmingly, we get to actually changing something and then bang – we hit the skids. 3D is all about making stuff happen. The next four sections expand on the 3D implementation philosophy and the nitty-gritty detail behind the philosophy. In particular the meaning of 'with agility'.

- **Using an Agile approach**

- **Benefits of Agile test and learn**

- **Loading the dice for success**

- **3R test framework**

Using an Agile approach

3D uses an Agile approach. What does agile mean? One definition of Agile with a capital A is: *'Agile project management is an iterative development methodology that values human communication and feedback, adapting to change, and producing working results.'* (Conrad, A. 2019)[2] Equally meaningful is the definition of agile with a small a: *'Able to move quickly and easily.'* (Oxford Lexico, 2019). The core concept behind an agile approach is to test and learn. We get going on each idea as soon as possible. In whatever order makes most sense. It's action-orientated. We don't batch up all our ideas into a monolithic block before doing anything. We act as soon as we can on each idea. And we test and learn.

This means that our design is likely to get implemented in stages. What can we do right now – this week – to start making our new design happen? It may be that some of the technical changes will take months. That's fine. What can we do in the meantime? And – just as important – build a better foundation for the technical components.

This test and learn approach is based on reality. Let's face it. We never really know how something new is going to work out until we try it. If it turns out as we'd hoped or better then we're in a good place. We've got some valuable learnings. We can proceed with the change with a justified confidence. If it turns out worse than we'd hoped then – oddly enough – we are still in a good place. We can use our learnings to modify the design and try again. Or, just as valuable, scrap the whole idea. Saving ourselves the large amount of time effort and money that a full-scale deployment would have cost. There's nothing new in a test and learn approach. Thomas Edison was one of the greatest inventors of all time. The electric lightbulb and the telephone were just two of his hundreds of inventions. To quote Edison: *'If I find 10,000 ways something won't work, I haven't failed. I am not discouraged, because every wrong attempt discarded is often a step forward.'* (Dyer, F. & Martin, T. 1910)[3]

We frequently test and learn in our daily lives. Often without even thinking about it. It's a natural response.

A great example is trying out a new cooking recipe. I'm in the kitchen making vegetable soup. I'm using a lentil base and decide to add some curry paste to give it a bit more kick. It's an improvement initiative – the kids found my earlier attempt a little bland. A bit boring, to quote them! I add some curry paste and have a little taste. Hmmm, can't really taste the difference. Add a bit more. No still not enough. A bit more. Aha perfect, just right! Better but needs more salt. Add a pinch of salt. Getting there. Doesn't look that great though. How about a drop of chilli-infused oil just to give it a bit of a sheen? Two more minutes on the hob to get it piping hot. One more taste. Perfect. 'Kids – lunch is ready.' 'Dad, this is delicious. You are a culinary genius!'

OK I made that last bit up. But you get the point. All I'm doing is continuous test and learn. And I'm iterating to a great result. In fact, each failure or learning point is not a failure at all. It's an essential step to the successful outcome.

I was at a Lean conference a few years ago. One of the guest speakers was Art Byrne. Art was CEO of Wiremold Ltd which was the lead case study used by Womack and Jones in their seminal book Lean Thinking. (Womack, J.P. & Jones, D.T. 2013)[4] As CEO of The Wiremold Company he quadrupled the company size and increased its enterprise value by a multiple of twenty-five in less than ten years. Wiremold outstripped its competitors on all fronts: productivity, profitability and growth.

By lucky accident we were next to each other in the queue for lunch. I grabbed the opportunity to have lunch with him and just ask questions and scribble his replies on napkins! My first question was: 'What are the top three factors you put down to your success with Lean?' Art replied (from memory): 'First, implement some or all of your new design immediately. Backfill the missing bits behind a curtain but show immediate action. Second, no sandbagging. People must say what they think they can achieve. Third, everyone must be hands-on. Everyone must be involved.'

I've never forgotten these three points. Especially the first word of Art's first point: 'Implement!'

Benefits of Agile test and learn

There are many advantages of an Agile test and learn approach. Here's my top five.

1. **Encourages action**

2. **Accelerates benefits**

3. **Iterates to the right answer**

4. **Reduces risks and costs**

5. **Drives bolder change**

Let's take a look at each one.

1. Encourages action. Test and learn helps us get going right away. It is the antidote to 'paralysis by analysis': Let's not do anything until we are one hundred per cent sure. Guess what? We are never one hundred per cent sure. So we don't do anything! Test and learn ensures we don't fall into this trap. To test means to take action. And action spawns more action. You can't steer a ship until you've got it underway. Does the initial direction have to be absolutely right? Not at all. As soon as we are underway, we can spin the wheel, trim the sails and make the necessary adjustments to our course. But only once we are underway.

2. Accelerates benefits. This spur to action means that we get benefits in the shortest possible time. These might be the benefits gained from the new solution working really well. Or the benefits from not wasting time and money on an idea that was never going to fly. Or the benefits of new learnings that we can put into the next iteration of our solution.

3. Iterates to the right answer. Have you noticed how you can only get so far trying to 'think' yourself to the perfect solution? Test and learn allows us to iterate to better and better solutions.

I want to improve my sitting room. It's all looking a bit tired. I can think and sketch and plan all I like. As soon as I start rearranging things I step back, look at it and think: 'There's something not quite right. Aha, the chair is too close to the door.' Move the chair. 'Actually, those pictures don't look so good side by side. I thought they'd look great but they don't.' Rearrange pictures. It's darker than I thought it would be. It needs some side lamps. Buy side lamps. A few iterations later – it's perfect. Da daaa! I love it.

But would I ever have got there, right first time, by thinking it all through to the ninth degree? No way. As human beings, we need to iterate.

4. Reduces risks and costs. Test and learn identifies problems early. This reduces risks and costs. Operational risk of accidents and injury. Market risk of litigation and reputational damage. Commercial risk of losing customers and exponential cost increases. It's a principle of new product development that the costs of fixing a problem increase exponentially, not linearly, with time. A simple example brings this to life.

Scenario one: A car manufacturer finds a fault in their brake liners during development testing. This is a standard situation. The test has done its job and it costs ten thousand dollars to revise the design and run another test.

Scenario two: The testing process is not thorough enough and the fault is missed. It is only discovered during final quality assurance ahead of production starting. Production plans are put on hold. The production delays, wasted inventory, expedited re-design and testing cost ten million dollars.

Scenario three: The final quality assurance tests are not thorough enough and the fault is missed. The car goes into production. It is a bestseller and a quarter of a million cars are sold in the first nine months. In month ten, instances of unexplained brake failures occur with three fatalities. There is an urgent recall. The costs of recall, fixing the problem and litigation are estimated at one billion dollars. This does not include the damage to the company reputation and its future prospects.

This example may be dramatic but it's not unrealistic. This article by Dan Burrows in Kiplinger 2018: '10 biggest product recalls of all time' provides a perspective.

Samsung had high hopes for the high-end Samsung Galaxy Note 7 smartphone, but they went up in smoke. The world's largest smartphone maker was forced to discontinue and recall the pricey gadget after some of them started bursting into flames. The US Consumer Products Safety Commission received ninety-six reports of overheating batteries and fires within the first two months of its August 2016 launch. Samsung was forced to recall two and a half million of the devices, which were some of the priciest smartphones on the market. The estimated cost was $5.3 billion. (Burrows, D. 2018)[5]

5. Drives bolder change. Stakeholders are more likely to support transformational change when it's positioned as test and learn. There is an understandable caution about approving big changes when it's a 'this is what we are going to do and there's no way back.' In these situations, a natural caution kicks in. Stakeholders try to minimise the changes in case something goes wrong. What could have been a transformational opportunity can too easily become a damp squib. For example, compare these two messages for transforming the rate of home security installations.

Message one: 'Hi everyone, we have a transformational solution for home security installations. The current customer waiting time is an average of three weeks with forty-three per cent no-shows when our engineer gets there. Our new solution enables same or next day installations. We have simulated our solution using the latest software and are confident it will work. We propose to move to this solution across the company from Monday 1st May. Please give this initiative your full support.'

Message two: *'Hi everyone, we believe we have a transformational solution to home security installations. The current customer waiting time is an average of three weeks with forty-three no-shows when our engineer gets there. Our new solution enables same or next day installations. We are proposing a test and learn approach starting with Engineering Team Six in the South West district. We will trial this for four weeks with this team and incorporate any learnings into our solution. All involved colleagues from operations, customer support, supply chain and field engineering are on board with this. And we have immediate rollback plans if it does not work as planned. We'd welcome your feedback and input into this plan including the trial planning.'*

Which one of these would you support? A likely reaction to the first message is: 'Whoa! Hold on. This is too risky. How about we try to gradually reduce the three weeks installation time to two weeks? Let's take a step-by-step approach.' The test and learn messaging is more palatable. It has made it much easier for cautious stakeholders to support a transformational design.

Loading the dice for success

In addition to adopting an Agile test and learn approach, there are a number of other things that we can do to load the dice in favour of successful implementation. Here are five recommendations based on personal experience.

1. **Keep the improvement team involved**

2. **Use test cells**

3. **De-couple as feasible**

4. **Focus on the next step**

5. **Set the right expectations**

Let's look at each in turn.

1. Keep the improvement team involved. Keep the front-line colleagues who were part of the improvement team involved in the implementation of their improvement ideas. It maintains ownership from start to finish. Be wary of the scenario where the improvement team throws everything over the wall to a new implementation team. In my experience, this just doesn't work. Neither team takes ownership. The improvement team dust off their hands and say, 'Job done! We've succeeded. Onto the next.' The project implementation team say, 'Hold on a minute! These improvement ideas won't work. We can't commit to deliver something we don't agree with.' It's a simple fix: Keep the improvement team involved until all or most of the improvement ideas are implemented.

2. Use test cells. The test cell concept is to start flowing small amounts of real work through a trial version of the new design as soon as feasible. This trial version typically includes first iterations of the non-technical and quick technical improvements. A team is selected to work in the test cell. The message to the test cell team is: 'Here's our new design. It's probably seventy to eighty per cent right. Your job is to prove it and improve it. The goal is to learn as much as possible as fast as possible by 'doing'. Make regular improvements on a daily or weekly basis and test the results. Measure the lead time and the process time for each unit of work and chart the results over the next month. Recommend other performance measures as you see fit. Capture all issues and make recommendations to solve them. We will meet daily to review the new design performance, issue resolution and how we implement your improvement recommendations.'

The test cell is a continual call to action. It takes us away from the end of the rainbow perfect solution scenario: always just round the corner. It makes us think pragmatically and creatively. 'OK, so you're saying we could get eighty per cent of the solution in a week by using PDFs and text messaging. Or wait three months for a one hundred per cent solution in our next system release. Let's go with the eighty per cent in our test cell next week.'

3. De-couple as feasible. Some improvements will be genuinely dependent on others. We can't do B until we've done A. But many will not. With a bit of imagination it's almost always possible to progress each improvement idea on its own merits. Why de-couple in this way? Because it maintains speed action and energy. Each improvement idea leader can get on and start testing and implementing their idea.

4. Focus on the next action. In his bestselling book on personal productivity, *Getting Things Done: The Art of Stress Free Productivity (Allen, D. 2015)*[6], David Allen lays out a common-sense and highly effective framework for – as the title says – getting things done. One of the pieces of advice that I personally found most helpful was: 'Just focus on "what's the next action?"' To quote: *'When a culture adopts "What's the next action?" as a standard operating query, there's an automatic increase in energy, productivity, clarity and focus.'* I use that advice every day in multiple different ways. For me it's transformational. Yet it's so basic and simple. In one sense, that's all we can actually do. The next action. We can't do the action after the next action until we've done the next action.

A Swiss technology company wanted to improve its E2E sales process. The colleagues that I was working with had a very detailed and diligent mindset. They liked everything to be just so. We were having an implementation workshop to discuss and agree the way forward on about twelve implementation ideas. And we were getting stuck. People were getting bogged down in over-engineered plans for each idea. It was all looking a bit impossible. I could feel the energy draining out of the room. Time for an intervention.

'OK,' I said. 'I'd like to go round the room and for everyone to share the next action for their improvement idea. The next action and the date for their next action. That's all. Just the next action and the date.' We went round the room and in ten minutes we had a flipchart listing Owner, Next Action and Date for each idea. All of them were within five days. All were eminently do-able. The energy and the buzz was back. We were underway.

5. Set the right expectations. Taking a test and learn approach allows you to set the right expectations with colleagues and stakeholders. It builds their participation and support. We all prefer something that we've been part of building. Here's the dialogue: 'Hi everyone, we've got an idea to improve things that we think will work well. However, the reality is that it might not. It might fail. So we're going to test it and learn as much as possible. And then we're going to use those learnings to either roll it out with confidence or improve the idea and try again or discard it as a valuable lesson learnt for next time. We'll be asking some of you to help us with this test and to contribute your expertise to the outcome. Thank you.'

People will react positively to this message and approach. It's humble. It's practical. It's respectful to the expertise and input that others have to bring to the table. It also sets you up for success whatever the outcome. If it's one hundred per cent right first time, 'Wow that's great. I guess we got lucky.' If it's seventy per cent right, it's as predicted and a great opportunity for colleagues to share their feedback and input. If it fails altogether, that's fine too. You made it clear that it was a test. You have the headroom to either improve the idea or try something different.

3R test framework

While Agile test and learn is fast and iterative, it's not a free for all. That would be counterproductive. Our tests need to be well organised and carefully managed. They need to give a useful outcome whether they succeed or fail. There's no point running a test just to say at the end of it: 'I can't quite see what the point of that was? We haven't learnt anything new!'

The starting point is to be clear about what we are testing for. What is our hypothesis? We do it all the time often without thinking. 'If I add some more salt to this lasagne it will taste better.' We can also add some simple measurements to our hypotheses to help determine the outcome. 'If I have a conversation with one new prospect each day then I'll make twice as many sales.' 'If I exercise each day for fourteen minutes then I will get fitter and achieve my target weight of seventy-six kilograms.'

We use exactly the same thinking for our process improvement tests. 'If we install customer home security units on the same or next day as the initial customer conversation, then our failed appointments, where customers are not at home, will fall from the current forty per cent to ten per cent.' We can have several closely related hypotheses. 'If we install customer home security units on the same or next day then our customer satisfaction scores will increase from the current thirty per cent to over eighty per cent.'

3D uses a simple framework called the 3Rs to help organise good tests. The 3Rs are Representative, Realistic and Risk. They each ask a key question.

1. Representative. 'Does this test cover a representative sample?' Typical considerations are customer types, gender, geography, seasonality, weather conditions, timing, complexity, type of product and service.

2. Realistic. 'Can we feasibly complete the scope of the test?' Typical considerations are timeline, resource availability, resource capability and volumes.

3. Risk. 'Does this test carry significant risk?' Typical considerations are operational risk, customer satisfaction and retention, financial loss, market risk, brand and reputational damage.

It is important to find the right balance of the 3Rs to have an effective test. The 3Rs gives us a simple discipline to make sure that we consider a range of options. There's often no perfect right answer. We just need to have the right discussions. And arrive at a good balance of the three factors.

Let's work through a simple example to see how the 3Rs work in practice.

Magda is fed up with driving to work each day. It's stressful. It's tiring. And it's not productive time. Her proposed improvement is to start taking the train to work instead. Her hypothesis is: 'If I take the train to work it will be less stressful and more productive.' Her stress measure is how she feels at the end of the day. Her productivity measure is whether she can get her daily update report done on the train. She often has to do this in the evenings. Magda decides to test her hypothesis using the 3R framework. The decision will only make sense financially if she buys an Annual Rail Travel Card. This is a significant financial outlay. She needs to feel confident in her decision before buying the card.

*- **Representative:** She decides to test taking the train for two weeks. That should be representative in terms of variations between weekdays and general travel issues. She's heard that the train is often more crowded on Friday than on the other weekdays. So she wants to travel on at least two Fridays.*

*- **Realistic:** She feels that this is a realistic and do-able test. The only problem is that she needs to do a school drop on Mondays and Fridays*

on the way to the station. This means she'll need to get a later train on those days.

- **Risk:** There is an increased risk of being late for work if there are any cancelled or late running trains. This is a particular concern on Wednesday – the day of her weekly leadership team meeting. She decides that this is an acceptable risk. Her deputy Mohamed can always chair the Wednesday meeting if necessary.

Outcome: Magda is happy with the results of the test and decides to switch to the train. It's also generated some useful learnings which she uses to further refine her plan. Getting the later train into work on a Friday is a bad option. It's much busier than on the other weekdays and she didn't get a seat at all on the second Friday and had to stand. She contacts the other parents and switches her school drop-off days to Monday and Thursday. In addition, she decides to get an earlier train both ways on Friday to avoid the rush hour. This also gets the weekend off to a kick start. The kids love it. She also gets the earlier train into work on Wednesday. This gets her to the office thirty minutes earlier and she appreciates the extra time to prepare for her weekly leadership meeting.

Magda extends the test by a third week to incorporate and test the iterative improvements: the earlier train on Wednesday and Friday and the Thursday school drop-off. It all works fine. She finds the train journey home a perfect time to write and send out her daily update report. This means that she switches off completely as soon as she gets home. She can just relax and enjoy family time.

She is finding it easier to socialise with her colleagues after work. Knowing that she can take the train rather than drive. Building some new relationships is an unexpected benefit.

The simple example demonstrates how the 3R framework puts a light touch rigour around a test while keeping it flexible and responsive to outcomes.

Here's a real-life case study that demonstrates the 3Rs in action. Notice how the test and learn approach helped challenge the current leadership thinking in a way that was both acceptable and conclusive.

In trying to increase their sales conversion and better utilise their capacity, a home appliance insurer would try to contact new customer leads up to twelve times over the first seventy-two hours. With fresh eyes, this felt excessive and could annoy potential customers. We challenged the team on why they took such a pushy sales style. 'Our leaders believe that the more we try and contact customers, the more sales we will make' was the response.

We decided to put this leadership thinking to the test using a data-driven approach. Our hypothesis, based on previous data, was that ninety-five per cent of new customer sales were made if you successfully contacted the potential customer within five attempts. The leadership team were interested but not fully convinced by the analysis. So we created a test cell with a sub-section of colleagues where we would call customers up to five times versus twelve times, and test in real-time whether our hypothesis was correct – utilising the 3Rs of testing (Representative, Realistic and Risk).

The test was a success. The test cell contacting potential customers up to five times made just as many sales as those using significantly more capacity to contact potential customer up to twelve times. This was a welcome revelation for the leadership team. It enabled them to increase overall sales by using the freed up capacity to cover more leads.

Continuously improving the process

Imagine that you've spent a weekend doing the garden. The flowers are blooming. It's a tapestry of colour and beauty. New shrubs and perennials planted. Expert pruning. Not a weed in sight. Soil fertilised and watered. Lawn mowed. Everything perfect. Spick and span.

You then go away on holiday for a few weeks. Would you expect it to look the same when you come back? I don't think so. If you did you'd be disappointed. Weeds will have returned. The lawn will be overgrown. Shrubs and flowers will need pruning. That's just life.

1. Process maintenance and improvement

Processes are exactly the same. They continually deteriorate without attention. Demand fluctuations, reorganisations, policy changes, additional measures and workarounds. The reality is that processes receive a constant battering! This isn't bad news. It just is. The solution is to continually improve our processes as a standard way of working. This is our natural practice with gardening. We don't give it a second thought. It's just what we do. 3D takes this same approach with three light touch actions.

1. Name the owner and team

2. Make it visible

3. Plug into the mains

Let's look at each in turn.

1. Name the owner and team. The team is a continual entity as part of daily working. It includes several roles.

- **Process owner:** this should be a senior leader in the organisation. Someone with enough clout to get the different functions working together to produce a great outcome.

- **Work experts:** one person from each area involved in the process. A process involving sales, service, operations, credit and finance would have a team of five. The main qualifications are that they are experts in their work and passionate about the process.

- **Process team leader:** this can be a rotating role so everyone gets the experience and development opportunity.

- **3D champion:** one colleague, who is familiar with 3D principles, to be the go-to person for the work expert team.

The team will be able to handle many of the day-to-day issues themselves. However, there will be times when they need some extra input, perhaps to facilitate a working session or suggest some additional ways to remove waste. The 3D champion is their specialist resource.

Between them the team has expertise in every part of the process. The team gets together at appropriate time frames to track how well the process is doing and to log issues and new improvement ideas. Keep it as light touch as possible. The main thing is to establish a regular rhythm. Perhaps start with a weekly thirty-minute call and iterate from there.

2. Make it visible. Building an end-to-end culture requires visibility of what's happening. Remember the proverb: 'Out of sight, out of mind.' It's true! One way to ensure visibility is to design a one-page poster for the process. The main thing is to keep it to one page and make it visual and interesting. It should be designed by the team. Put it somewhere where everyone can easily see it. Both physically and virtually.

Recommended poster content includes photographs, vision, measures, performance and hot news. Photographs of the process owner, the work experts team and the 3D champion. Have name and role under each photograph. The photographs make it personal and real. It's not an abstract concept. This is the team that's making it an amazing process. Have the vision in big bold lettering. Add the measures that are being used to evaluate the process performance. Keep to three maximum. Less is more. Show the performance over a meaningful timescale so that people can see the trend. Finally have a hot news section such as successes, new initiatives and customer feedback. Keep the poster up to date. It should be a key output of the process team's regular connect.

Please see an illustration of a poster for an E2E recruitment process in Figure 4.10. The team have put it on the intranet.

3. Plug into the mains. Embed your continuous improvement into the fabric of the organisation. It's not something special on the side. It's part of daily running. The owner and the team need to feel accountable as part of day-to-day working. One easy way to do this is to include quick five-minute updates as part of standard agenda items in the normal schedule of meetings. This moves end-to-end performance from being something special – project-based – to part of day-to-day working – culture-based.

The sponsor, owner and each member of the end-to-end team should have something in their goals relating to the performance of the end-to-end process. This doesn't need to be over-engineered but it does need to be there in some shape or form. This is what makes it real.

2. Why this sustainability approach works

Organisations often struggle with continuous improvement of their processes. A typical pattern is that there's an improvement project. Things improve. And then the process slowly deteriorates. No one really notices. And when they do there's no one available to jump in and fix it. The above approach provides an antidote to this situation. It brings three essential factors to the table:

1. The team is in place. It's a team with the right mix of skills and capabilities to address problems. It's connecting on a regular basis. And it's a team of people who feel accountable. Any E2E continuous improvement initiative that doesn't include a named team is doomed to failure. Why? Because it means that when there are problems and issues — and there will be – a new team has to be formed. And that makes it a project team. Exactly what we want to avoid.

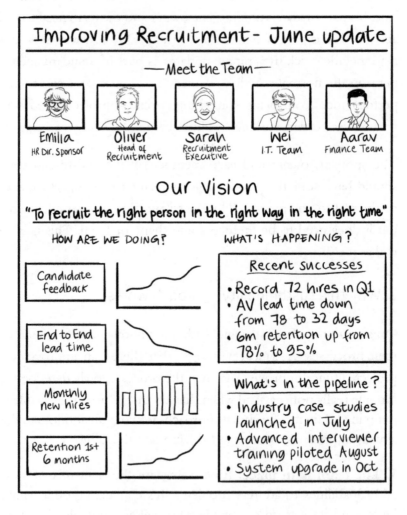

Figure 4.10 E2E Poster example

2. Performance and accountability are visible. The one-page visual shines a light on what's happening. And – just as importantly – who is responsible for making it happen. It keeps it front of mind. It's light touch and easy to maintain. One page means bad news can't be buried as a footnote to Appendix 7!

3. It's part of daily work. This is key. There's nothing special or one-off with this approach. A focus on E2E process performance together with the capability to make it happen is embedded into the culture of the organisation.

A glass manufacturing company was deploying 3D. They did six E2E improvements of their most important processes in the first year. A key outcome of each improvement was not just the streamlined process but the named continuous improvement team and the one-page visual.

We had a regular slot, once a quarter, at the senior leadership team meeting. Part of our update was running through the one-page visuals for each E2E process. Some took less than a minute. Others took longer when there was a particular issue or point of discussion.

This light touch format did its job. It kept E2E performance front of mind. It enabled constructive interventions by the leadership team when necessary. And it boosted the expert work team members to know their efforts were recognised.

Benefits of End-to-End

The E2E dimension delivers many benefits. Some obvious, some more subtle.

1. The obvious benefits

Happier customers. The entire process has been designed around the customer and what they want to achieve from the process. Right first time, faster, less effort, more reliable, safer. Whatever is relevant to the customer outcome.

Personal fulfilment. It's much more satisfying working with elegant and effective processes that delight our customers. It just feels good. It generates success, positive feedback and recognition.

Scalability for growth. I often hear comments like: 'Our broken processes mean we just can't scale. If we double our revenues, we double our costs.' Streamlined processes provide a bedrock for scalable and profitable growth.

Enables new partnerships. It's easier for new partners to connect into transparent and effective processes. It also makes the organisation more attractive to potential new partners.

Continual improvement. Streamlined visible processes are – paradoxically – easier to improve than broken processes. You can see what's going on. Problems and opportunities are more obvious. They provide greater opportunity for technologies like automation, data analytics and artificial intelligence. Robotics is a good example. There's no point in automating a broken process. All we'd be doing is to speed up and lock in the waste.

Increases revenues. Happier customers translate into revenue growth. Higher retention of existing customers plus new customers through digital media and word of mouth.

Reduces costs. Waste always carries some sort of costs. I often say: 'Better processes cost less not more.' Defects, rework, over-engineering, over-production, inventory and delays have all been targeted and removed – or at least significantly reduced – as part of the new design.

Increases profits. A natural outcome of revenue growth and cost reduction.

2. The less obvious benefits

These stories help illustrate and bring to life the more subtle benefits of E2E improvements.

Helps optimise the whole. What happens when people can see their part of the process but not the whole picture? *As part of an improvement initiative at a hydropower generation company the team went on site visits to see the dams in action. At one dam, the colleagues were upbeat that on that day they had taken the initiative to optimise their dam. They'd seen that plenty of rain was forecast so rather than build the water up in the reservoir as instructed they released it down the river, knowing it would quickly fill back up with the rain.*

Unfortunately, they hadn't considered the bigger picture. Electricity prices were actually going to be much higher the next day as some coal stations were down and it wasn't going to be so windy. Also, releasing the water had a negative knock-on impact on dams further downriver. When we went through this with them and their colleagues at Head Office, it became clear that there was a real opportunity to improve by making sure that everyone was aware of the big picture at all times. This included more clearly defined roles and responsibilities and a better understanding of how each position fitted into the overall process. This enabled the teams to work better together and optimise the output for the entire hydropower system.

Supports technology initiatives. Technology can only help when the process works. *A client had just implemented a workflow solution for its complaints handling process. Unfortunately it was not delivering the expected benefits. Just the opposite – everything was taking longer. People were working with the old manual system, printing and moving paper between teams as before, and updating the new workflow system as an additional activity!*

An E2E initiative was launched to fix the problem. It turned out that the workflow system was missing three key pieces of information created at different stages in the E2E process. The only way to get this information was to print and move paper from team to team as before. It was an obvious fix. The workflow system was modified, the manual workaround became unnecessary and the anticipated benefits started flowing. The E2E initiative had provided the bedrock for the technology to work.

Brings unexpected benefits. The reality is that we never really know all the benefits until the process is improved and running. Often all sorts of positive things start happening that we could never have predicted in advance. This case study illustrates the point.

I led an E2E improvement of the Baringa recruitment process. We'd decided this was a top priority. The organisation was growing at around twenty per cent per year, the competition for top talent was intense and the current process was clunky and slow. Lead times were long and unpredictable and the candidate experience was average. Using the E2E approach, we redesigned and implemented the new process in two months.

There were a whole series of improvements covering roles and responsibilities, target lead times, form design, training and the interview process itself. The result was a faster and more transparent and enjoyable process for the candidate with rapid feedback after each interview. So far so good. Much as expected.

Then some unexpected benefits started to come in. The average lead time from first contact to offer accepted shrunk from seventy to twenty-seven days. Our target had been forty days but the new process just worked better and faster than expected. Glassdoor.com is a website where people can post their feedback on their experience with organisations. The feedback on the Baringa recruitment process became very positive in terms of speed, rapid feedback and overall friendliness. This often influenced candidates with two or three job offers towards joining Baringa. The percentage of offers accepted to offers made jumped from seventy-two per cent to eighty-nine per cent. This single change made a big difference to our ability to grow. Could anyone have predicted that at the start, or built a business case on it? Absolutely not. It was a nice surprise!

1 Birkett, A. (2019, June). Form Design: 13 Empirically Backed Best Practices. CXL.Com. https://cxl.com/blog/form-design-best-practices/

2 Conrad, A. (2019, November). What Exactly Is Agile? A Definition of Agile Project Management. Blog.Capterra.Com. https://blog.capterra.com/definition-of-agile-project-management/

3 Dyer, F. L., & Martin, T. C. (1910). Edison: His Life and Inventions (Vol. 2). Harper & Brothers, New York.

4 Womack, J. P., & Jones, D. T. (2013). Lean Thinking. Simon & Schuster.

5 Burrows, D. (2018, March). 10 Biggest Product Recalls of All Time. Https://Www.Kiplinger.Com. https://www.kiplinger.com/slideshow/investing/t052-s000-10-biggest-product-recalls-of-all-time/index.html

6 Allen, D. (2015). Getting Things Done: The Art of Stress-Free Productivity (Revised ed.). Penguin Books.

Part Five

THE AGAIN-AND-AGAIN DIMENSION

Constancy does not begin but is that which perseveres.

- Leonardo da Vinci

Again-and-Again overview

3D makes sustainability an integral part of the approach – not a factor on the side. To repeat what I said earlier: *'By the time you need to start worrying about sustainability it's too late!'* AAA puts the spotlight on sustainability from the start and keeps it there. It is always front of mind. A kind of positive paranoia. Sustaining 3D ways of working is not an afterthought. Or a separate initiative. It is embedded into every fibre of the approach.

The aim of the AAA dimension is to heavily stack the odds on the side of sustainability. The AAA Five Questions Checklist synthesises years of experience, good and bad, into what works and doesn't work in sustaining a continuous improvement way of working. Executing the checklist does not mean that there will never be sustainability challenges. There are always sustainability challenges. It means that the capability and culture will be rugged, robust and resilient enough to handle those challenges. A good analogy is a sailing boat at sea. There will always be storms. But a well-built boat can weather those storms.

The leadership of an organisation has an especially important role to play in the AAA dimension. AAA is a powerful and proven way to embed a continuous improvement culture in the organisation. But it requires the commitment of leadership to do it. As we go through each checklist point, we'll see how this commitment is translated into a series of clear-cut leadership decisions. These decisions are where the rubber hits the road.

Why Again-and-Again is important

AAA is perhaps the most important of the three dimensions. If a team experiences some lumps and bumps using TBT ways of working, we can ask why, address the issues and use the learnings for other teams. If an E2E initiative stalls or fails, again we can ask why and use it as a learning experience to refine our approach. But if the entire improvement agenda fails or stalls, then where do we go from there? It gets a bad name. It's closed down. Another initiative that's failed. Everything goes quiet for a year. Then a new initiative is launched and the same cycle is repeated. The amount of waste involved is staggering.

TBT and E2E support each other in many ways as explained in section: **End-to-End and Team-by-Team working together**. However, by themselves, they are not enough. Adopting 3D is not a once-off or a one- or two- or three-year initiative. It's a continuance. Otherwise it's just another form of waste. Another failed initiative. This is the purpose of the third dimension AAA. To embed continuous improvement into the culture of your organisation as a continuance.

Again-and-Again Five Questions Checklist

Here is the AAA Five Questions Checklist. It has been developed from years of seeing what works – and just as important, what doesn't work – in terms of sustainability.

1. **Is leadership engaged and participating?**

2. **What is our capability building goal, plan and progress?**

3. **Are we working on the right things at the right pace?**

4. **How do we embed a culture of continuous improvement?**

5. **What is our 3D Centre?**

Effective delivery of each point is as important as the points themselves. It is not just what to do, but how to do it. 3D brings proven and practical ways to make each point happen.

1. Is leadership engaged and participating?

Get this one right and it provides the foundation for sustainability. Get it wrong and we are building on sand.

Most leaders want to engage, support and participate in improvement initiatives. But I've noticed three factors which can act as inhibitors.

- Bad experience. They've had bad experiences with previous initiatives that didn't work. I've frequently heard comments such as: 'We tried that improvement stuff at my last organisation. It failed. Lots of experts with martial art titles and complex statistical tools. Too slow. Too specialist.'

- Don't know how. They don't have a clear view on how to help. No one has answered their question 'I want to help. So what do I need to do differently to support this initiative? Give me a practical hands-on way to help. No theories. No deep statistics that I'll never use. Just a list of things I can personally do that will make a big difference fast.'

- Too fragmented. Leadership support has been fragmented. It doesn't work to get leaders engaged one at a time. It has to be as a community. This first checklist question needs a further build: **'Is leadership engaged and participating as a community?'** It's no use having one leader supportive while their colleagues are standing on the sidelines. What's needed is a way to get the entire leadership community on board fast! Within days and weeks – not months.

How to do this? To help answer this question we developed the 3D leadership course and coaching programme. It's not about leadership in general. It's specific: What do I need to do as a leader in my organisation to support, engage and participate in embedding continuous improvement into our culture? You can download the objectives and agenda of the course and coaching from **the3dworkplace.com**. Over the past five years it has been delivered to hundreds of leadership teams and communities. It does five things.

- Gets leadership teams engaged as a community.

- Puts the key decisions to make on the table.

- Triggers open discussion and action around those decisions.

- Supports each leader in their personal development.

- Embeds leadership engagement into daily working culture.

This case study demonstrates typical outcomes.

A continuous improvement initiative at a global bank was stalling. The improvement teams were complaining that they had little or no support from leadership. One of the team told me: 'I'm spending seventy per cent of my time convincing stakeholders that the initiative is worth doing and thirty per cent actually improving things!' Another team member told me: 'My sponsor won't meet with me. I think he's nervous that our improvement work will show him up.'

To turn this around, we were brought in to deliver the 3D leadership course to multiple leadership teams across the bank. Retail, commercial, cards, mortgages, operations, HR, finance, legal and IT. For many of the teams it was the first time that they had discussed their role in leading continuous improvement as a team. This last point 'as a team' is the key. Once they started discussing it, they quickly realised the impact that they could deliver with some relatively simple actions and decisions. 'Why wouldn't we do this?' was an oft-heard comment.

Attendees were frequently surprised by the simplicity of the actions that they were being asked to do. Many had been put off by complicated statistical techniques and specialist jargon in previous careers. And they'd seen them fail. 3D made sense for them in day-to-day actions.

Leadership teams became aware of the waste that they themselves were creating for their people. The course provided a safe environment to discuss it and what they could do differently to remove it. The courses and follow-up coaching generated a positive reaction from the improvement colleagues on the ground. 'Now I can get to meet with my stakeholders the same day. It's clear that my work is a priority for them.'

Contrast the speed and momentum of the above with the traditional one-stakeholder-at-a-time approach.

I was attending a conference on operational excellence. We'd broken into groups to discuss particular issues. I joined the table discussing 'Leadership Engagement'. The group facilitator worked for a global oil company. His job title was Head of Stakeholder Engagement.

He told us how it worked. 'It's difficult making change happen in our organisation. It takes a long time and you have to get everybody on board. Everyone has to say yes but anyone can say no. Once we've agreed an initiative, my role is to identify a champion for the initiative. Then I work with the champion to test it out and prove the results. Depending on the outcomes, we then build up support around the champion.' I asked him how long this process usually took. 'Oh, we usually build up good momentum after a year or so,' he replied.

It sounds logical and sensible. It probably worked OK in the past. But in today's world it is just not fit for purpose. It's too slow. By the time good momentum has built up, half the people are in different roles. The head of a recruitment company told me that at any point in time eighty per cent of people are looking to move into new roles or leave the organisation. I can't vouch for its accuracy but it's a real wake-up call. Whatever we need to do to get everyone on board we need to do it fast.

The 3D leadership course and coaching programme are flexible. The balance of training and coaching flexes to what each leadership team decides is right for them. In the previous case study of the bank the emphasis was on a global roll-out of the leadership course. Here ia a case study of an organisation that went all in on the coaching.

A government agency had tried several approaches to improve performance over the years, the ghosts of many of them still around and with scary stories to match. They decided to take a different approach and to truly invest in the leadership and sustainment side of their transformation. It is easy to cut this piece out when budgets are tight and the value is harder to visualise. As well as delivering training on the methods and behaviours needed to be operationally excellent, the leadership made an investment of a sixteen-week coaching programme.

This was a different approach from previous initiatives with less classroom training and a greater focus on actually practising and implementing the changes. The outcome was an increase in both productivity and personal engagement scores. Most importantly, it changed the language and the day-to-day working culture of the organisation.

Of course this is just the start. Leadership engagement is a never-ending process. The remaining AAA Checklist Questions all play a part in embedding that engagement into the fabric of the organisation.

2. What is our capability building goal, plan and progress?

Capability used to be just a word for me. I'd throw it into discussions without much thought. That changed when I almost drowned. I think of this experience every time I say the word capability.

We were on a local boat trip around the coast of Zakynthos, in the Ionian Islands of Greece. We'd stopped at Navagio Beach, or Shipwreck Beach, an exposed cove where, in 1980, a ship ran aground during stormy weather and bad visibility. The ship was abandoned and still rests buried in the limestone gravel of the beach that now bears the nickname Shipwreck.

Our boat with twenty people on board including my wife and I anchored about two hundred yards from the beach. The captain announced this was as close as he could get in shallow water. About eight feet deep. Anyone who'd like to explore the beach and shipwreck should swim from here. Everyone dived overboard – including me – and swam for the beach. The problem was that I can't really swim any distance. I don't have the capability. I tell myself I do but in fact I don't. I'm fooling myself.

Halfway to the shore, in about seven feet of water, I panicked and went into a rapid negative spiral. I couldn't breathe. My chest was constricted. I started swallowing water. My wife tried to hold me up but didn't have the strength. She shouted for help. Two boys on the shore heard her call and ploughed out to me. They were exceptional swimmers and reached me in about thirty seconds. They each grabbed an arm and towed me to the beach on my back. I'd turned blue. It took me about an hour to slowly recover in the warm Greek sun. Those two boys saved my life. I've no doubt about it.

I'm not proud of this story. But it changed my view on what capability really means. And the importance of achieving the necessary capability in any endeavour. 3D adopts three principles to achieve the necessary capability.

1. **Aim for the heart.**

2. **Use an objective framework to measure capability.**

3. **Agree clear goals based on this framework.**

1. Aim for the heart

Embedding 3D as a way of working requires a new level of capability in the organisation. These capabilities have been covered in **Part Three: The TBT Dimension** and **Part Four: The E2E Dimension.** 3D is easy to learn but it does need to be learnt. This capability can't be theoretical. It has to be practical and proven. Capability needs to be embedded into the heart of the organisation – to the people who do the work. Not just a team of specialists on the outside.

Why is this so important? This case study helps explain.

A telecommunications company had been running an operational excellence programme for three years. It had built up a central team of twenty five improvement experts. The approach was to plant a team of two to three experts into a business area. They would work with a small group of colleagues from the business, usually three to five strong, and the joint team would do the improvement to the business. A typical result was a fifteen to twenty per cent increase in productivity and a better service to customers. Each initiative was seen as a project.

During the improvement project, the front-line colleagues who had been seconded into the project team often worked twelve-to-fourteen-hour days. They had their day jobs as well as the project work. It was PowerPoint heavy. Immaculate fifty-page PowerPoint decks, taking days to produce, to get through a one hour checkpoint were the norm.

After three years the business had got fatigue. They were tired of having the improvement done to them. A new CEO came in, listened to the business and closed the programme down. Within a few months there was hardly a trace of the programme. Most of the experts left. The remainder moved into different roles. I knew many people involved in the programme and asked them why it had lacked sustainability and evaporated so quickly. They emphasised one reason above all others. A failure to build and embed capability into the front line: the people actually doing the work.

When capability is embedded into the heart of the organisation it becomes a part of the culture. It's just what people do. It's how we work together.

2. Use an objective framework to measure capability

It is essential to have an objective framework against which to measure your capability building.

For example, if I was to tell you I'm an accountant you might quite reasonably expect me – in the UK – to be a certified member of the Association of Chartered Accountants (ACA) or an equivalent organisation in other countries. In this situation, the ACA and its accreditation system, is providing an objective and accepted competency framework against which to measure my skills. If I was to tell you that I'm an accountant but I don't have any qualification – I've just decided that I'm an accountant – you might be less than impressed.

3D uses the Lean Competency System to provide this objective yardstick. The Lean Competency System (LCS) is a globally recognised competency framework and is used by hundreds of organisations and tens of thousands of individuals worldwide. Created in 2005 by the Lean Enterprise Research Centre, Cardiff Business School, it is managed by Lean Competency Services Ltd under licence from Cardiff University. The LCS provides Lean qualifications for individuals, consultants and organisations. Go to **leancompetency.org** for full details of the LCS organisation and competency framework.

Simon Elias is Head of the Lean Competency System and has led it since its inception. Here is Simon's vision for the LCS: *'To promote and accelerate the adoption of Lean thinking in organisations, so they become more effective in achieving their purpose. It's also about fostering engagement by providing a development framework for practitioners, so they can continuously learn and improve their capabilities and at the same time receive recognition and reward for their capabilities.' (Elias, S. 2022).*

LCS competency levels. The LCS framework has seven levels of competency covering the entire spectrum of Lean knowledge and application. They are grouped into three categories: Fundamental, Technical and Strategic. You can read a full description of the framework on the LCS website.

There are three levels in particular that form the core of capability building in a 3D initiative. LCS Level 1a is for everyone involved. It means understanding the underlying principles of Lean, its development and antecedents. LCS Level 1c is for team leaders and subject matter experts. It means understanding and demonstrating proven delivery of the tools and techniques required to apply and sustain Lean in the workplace. LCS Level 2a is for initiative leaders on the ground. It means deploying the advanced Lean knowledge and leadership competencies required for Lean management.

Having the ability to design and implement programmes and play a leading role in managing departmental or cross-functional teams with some support and guidance.

Why the Lean Competency System? There are several reasons why the 3D development team decided to work with the LCS competency framework over other alternatives.

- Focuses on the individual. LCS focuses on the individual as well as the organisation. A favourite part of my job is to facilitate the LCS accreditation interviews and exams of my client colleagues. I am always amazed by the depth and speed of their new learning and capabilities. Their passion and enthusiasm. And the impact it is having on their organisations. Achieving a LCS accreditation is good for people's career. It is an internationally recognised certification. It answers the question: 'What's in it for me?'

- Unleashes hidden talent. Through its globally recognised framework and action-orientated approach, LCS gives people a way to shine, show their true potential and accelerate their career. Colleagues whose potential and talent might otherwise go unnoticed.

A global consumer products company launched a process simplification programme with a strong focus on building an internal capability using the Lean Competency System framework. To help scale the programme and sustain change, they created a network of Lean champions comprising individuals from across the business who showed a keen interest in LCS and demonstrated their capability in delivering their own team-based improvement.

They knew from experience that providing an externally recognised accreditation would be a real draw for ambitious talent, but what they had not anticipated was just how much untapped talent would be revealed! One great example was Sophie who worked on the service desk and was relatively unknown as an up-and-coming talent. Within six months that had all changed. She had presented on multiple improvement topics to the COO who now knew her personally and referenced her as a leading light for the initiative.

- Measures true people capability. It's not theoretical or conceptual. It names people with proven competency. LCS provides an objective measure of the actionable Lean improvement capability in the organisation. Here's a typical, if slightly idealistic, scenario.

Our organisation is one hundred people strong. Everyone knows the fundamental principles of Lean and has achieved their LCS Level 1a accreditation. The whole organisation understands the basic Lean principles of making work work better. We have a common language around customer value and waste. Twenty colleagues have demonstrated how they use Lean principles and methods to improve their teams' daily ways of working and certain processes that had not been working well. They've achieved their LCS Level 1c accreditation based on their new skills and proof of the positive impact they have had in their areas. Three colleagues enjoy the improvement work so much that they've asked to make it at least half of their job. They have achieved their LCS Level 2a accreditation and become the go-to people for leading new initiatives and training colleagues and new joiners.

What is the point of this simple example? That the LCS framework has given us an objective measurement of the new capability in the organisation.

- Action-orientated. In the above scenario, the new capability is making a real difference on the ground day-in day-out. To quote from the LCS website: *'Competency has two dimensions: knowledge and application, both of which have to be demonstrated in LCS Assessments.'* This means that action, outcomes and tangible benefits are required to achieve any certification beyond LCS Level 1a.

Please see an illustration of a LCS Accreditation Award event in Figure 5.1. The five colleagues are being awarded their official LCS Certificates. The leadership team has taken the oppotunity to attend and recognise their achievement.

3. Agree clear goals

A simple way to develop your 3D capability is to answer these three questions:

1. **What's our capability goal?**

2. **What's our plan to achieve this goal?**

3. **How are we doing?**

Let's look at each question in turn.

1. What's our capability goal? It's important to have a clear objective in mind. It might take a few weeks and months but the goal should be clear. It is seldom about mass sheep dipping. Focusing on an outcome triggers a subset of helpful questions. Who do we want to have a basic understanding of Lean improvement principles? Who should understand and use TBT ways of working? Who will lead our E2E process improvements? Who could be part of our 3D Champion community? Who in the organisation could lead our capability building plan? Answering these questions will develop the target outcome.

2. What's our plan to achieve this goal? Capability building should follow and support the plan to get started. See section: **Getting started – let's go!** for the various alternatives. So if you've decided to roll out TBT ways of working across your organisation

Figure 5.1 LCS Awards ceremony

then TBT training will probably take first priority. If you've decided to improve five core E2E processes as the first step, then it makes sense to start with E2E training for the teams involved. Another option is to up-skill the leadership community as the first step. That way leadership is engaged, participating and supporting from the get-go. Two key principles are 'just-in-time' and 'learning-by-doing'. This is why the capability plan should support and follow the getting started plan.

3. How are we doing? The LCS Competency Framework provides an objective way to answer this question. As we saw earlier, 3D deployments tend to concentrate around three of the seven LCS competency levels: LCS Levels 1a, 1c and 2a. These three levels provide a solid foundation for building proven, actionable and effective capability.

Let's finish with a case study that shows how 3D and LCS work together to embed a new capability and culture across an organisation.

I was working with the COO of a trading company to establish their continuous improvement capability and culture. They had selected 3D as the backbone of their approach. Her mantra was: 'We want to move to a place where not everything has to be a project to get improved!'

The organisation in scope was about three hundred strong. Building and embedding a sustainable culture of continuous improvement was her priority goal. To this end and using the LCS Accreditation System, she designed and delivered the following plan. All colleagues were encouraged to attend the LCS Level 1a training eLearning or half-day course and get accredited. Around ten half-day courses were delivered in a two-month period covering some one hundred of the three hundred colleagues. The remainder chose the eLearning option. The COO made a short video explaining why the initiative was so important. The LCS Level 1a training got everyone on board and participating in three months. One exercise in the training was to identify waste in the attendees' own areas. Over two hundred opportunities were identified. A high point was the CEO who appeared on the company internal TV network waving his LCS Level 1a certificate with a big smile on his face.

The COO and her colleagues determined the right community for LCS Level 1c training and accreditation. This comprised the twenty-two team leaders, the eight strong change and project management group and fifteen subject matter experts. So a community of forty-five colleagues in total. The COO joined this group. At the end of six months, thirty-eight people were LCS Level 1c accredited and seven had dropped out for various reasons.

The COO set up a small group called the Operational Excellence (OE) Team to provide leadership and governance for the initiative. The team was led by a colleague with a natural combination of skills for the role. He was great at engaging stakeholders, a good team leader and very hands-on. The team's mandate was to get the initiative off the ground and embed continuous improvement into the culture. Then the team would dissolve back into the business or become even smaller. The initial size was the team leader plus three colleagues. All four achieved their LCS Level 2a accreditation over an eighteen-month period.

The combination of 3D and LCS embedded a new capability deep into the organisation. The numbers at the end of the first year were as follows.

- *Total number of colleagues: 300*
- *LCS Level 1a accredited: 272*
- *LCS Level 1c accredited: 38*
- *LCS Level 2a accredited: 5*

- *LCS Level 2b accredited: 2*
- *Total number of teams using TBT ways of working: 22*
- *Total number of E2E improvements: 8*

The COO's goal of moving to a place where not everything has to be a project to get improved had been achieved.

3. Are we working on the right things at the right pace?

Sustainability depends on having a real impact on the business. This means improving the things that count. No one's going to support an initiative that streamlines the canteen queueing times but ignores the order to cash process that underpins the business. That means having a simple way to prioritise what to work on.

1. Are we working on the right things?

The 3D team has developed a simple and intuitive tool to help you work on the right things and at the right pace. To support the planning and have the right discussions with your colleagues. It is called the Process Team Matrix (PTM). The PTM has the E2E process names down the left-hand side as rows and the team names across the top as columns. To the right of the E2E process names are columns for prioritisation criteria. Five typical criteria are the impact on customers, staff, revenues, costs and quality. Underneath the team names along the top is a row called priority. The PTM is - above all - a tool to generate the right discussions. A typical PTM completion exercise goes like this:

1. Discuss and agree that you have captured all the E2E processes and teams in scope.

2. Mark the teams that are in each process using an X at the intersection between the process and the team. This now gives you a visual picture of which teams are in which processes.

3. Discuss and complete the prioritisation columns for your E2E processes. I recommend keeping it simple using a priority one, two or three scoring system.

4. Give each team a priority score for up-skilling in TBT ways of
    working.

Let's just reflect on what we've accomplished in our PTM
working session. Agreed the processes and teams in scope.
Agreed the prioritisation criteria for our process improvement
work. Seen – often for the first time – a picture of which teams
are involved in which processes. Most importantly, we've agreed
the priority order for our TBT and E2E initiatives. And it's all on
one whiteboard or one page. When I say agreed, I mean had an
intense discussion and agreed. There is always a huge amount of
debate and challenge in these sessions. Brilliant! That's the whole
point. That's the real value.

Note that your PTM is a living diagram. It doesn't have to be
absolutely right. In fact, it never will be. It's a moving picture. The
only thing that needs to be right is what to get going on right away.
Your priority areas.

**Please see an example PTM for a Home Media company in
Figure 5.2**. The Priority Ones are to upskill Sales, Customer Service,
Finance and IT in TBT ways of working; and to improve the E2E
process: 'Winning sales to receiving payment.' The prioritisation
criteria have been omitted to keep it simple.

2. At the right pace?

Most organisations that I've worked with completely get the first
part of the question: **Are we working on the right things?** It's
the second part that causes problems: **At the right pace?** Here's an
example of a typical conversation.

*Q: What's your plan for continuous improvement in your
organisation?'*

*A: 'Oh we're clear on that. We want our core processes streamlined
and to solve problems as a way of working.'*

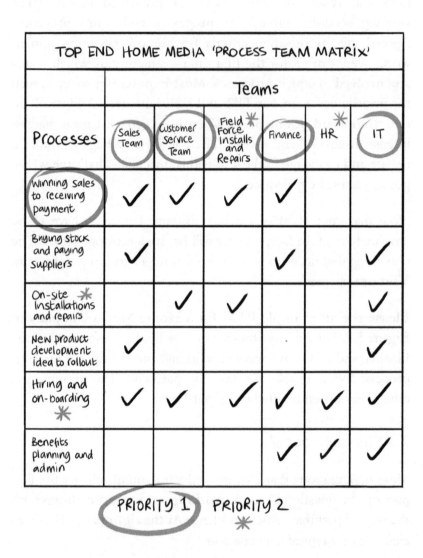

Figure 5.2 Process Team Matrix example

Q: 'That sounds great. How many processes and people are in scope?'

A: 'Around twenty core processes and four hundred people.'

Q: 'What's happening at the moment?'

A: 'It's going well. Last year we did our first core process improvement that delivered good benefits and won a lot of support for the initiative. This year we plan to do four more processes. In addition, we've plans to roll out TBT to the finance and HR teams. That's about eighty people.'

Q: 'What's your end goal?'

A: 'To embed a culture of continuous improvement across our whole organisation. It's a foundation pillar for our strategy.'

Q: 'And what's the timeline to achieve this?'

A: 'We don't have a specific date. But certainly within two years. This year we're still building support.'

What's the takeaway here? It's simple. The initiative is going too slow and too small scale to achieve its stated objective. It is not going to happen. So what will happen? In about twelve months or less someone on the leadership team is going to say: 'Hold on, it's not working! Sure there are some good things happening but nothing like the breadth and scale of impact that we need.' And the initiative will be quietly closed down or just fade away. Sustainability requires that we have the necessary size and scale of impact to achieve our goals.

Think of it as taking off in a jumbo jet. There's the period of taxiing down the runway. Next time you fly note how the pilot is testing the flaps and tailfins as they taxi to their take-off position. Then there's a few seconds while they rev up the engines with the breaks on. The engines scream. The aircraft shudders against its brakes. And then?

They go for it. Full power on all engines. Slowly at first, 10 mph, then faster 50 mph, then faster 100 mph, then really fast 170... 180... 184 mph... take-off speed... the front wheels lift up... then suddenly the jumbo is flying... climbing climbing climbing... within fifteen minutes you are at cruising altitude. And using a fraction of the fuel per mile than was used to take off. But now imagine that instead of going for it, the pilot gently revs up and trundles steadily down the runway. They comes on the address system: 'Hi everyone, your captain here. We'll be playing it safe today and staying at a level 70 mph all the way down the runway. It's the steady and measured way. Have a good flight!'

Of course, we know what will happen. It's not safer at all. In fact, we're going to crash! And yet this is what so often happens in improvement initiatives. The pace is too slow. The impact is too small. And it 'crashes'. So what's the answer? Another example points to the way:

Suppose I've asked you to mow my field and you've agreed. Next I ask you to tell me how long it's going to take you and what people and equipment you'll need? What would your response be? My guess is you'd say: 'How big is your field?' Any other response would almost certainly lead to trouble. If my field is five hundred square metres then one person with a small hand-pushed lawn mower should be fine for an afternoon's work. But if my field is a thousand-acre wheat prairie then that one person could work for ten years and not come close!

The size of the field and how fast we want to mow it is all important in determining what people and resources we need. In deciding our plan.

This is where the PTM proves itself exceptionally useful. It not only helps you decide what to work on but also at what pace. It shows you the size of the field on one page and drives all the right discussions. What do we want to work on first? How big is the total landscape? How long do we want to take to improve all the priority ones and twos? So what pace will we need to work at? Which teams will be involved in each process improvement? Do we want to up-skill these teams in TBT ways of working at the same time?

3. Hints and tips

Here are some hints and tips for making the PTM as helpful as possible.

Keep it simple. There's a natural tendency to make the PTM more and more sophisticated. A classic example is to add weightings to each of the prioritisation criteria and then calculate some sort of prioritisation score for each potential initiative. For example, the sales process scores 762, service process 698, and recruitment 632. That's fine but be careful. Time and again I've seen a list of scores where everyone present knew they were giving the wrong outcome. Agree to use numerical scores as helpful indicators. And that intuition and personal judgement will make the final decision.

Value sponsor support. Let's say there are two priority one processes, sales and service, and we can only proceed with one in the short term. Sales is clearly the highest value option but the sponsor is a bit lukewarm. Service is lower value but the sponsor is passionate and determined to make it a huge success. I'd go for service every time. Success feeds on success. Leave sales for the next round. By that time the sponsor will be thinking: 'I wish we'd gone first.'

Review and update monthly. Your PTM is not a photograph. It's a movie. Review and update it monthly. Keep it on your wall. Make it a discussion centrepiece. It will continually change and evolve. 'This is what we're working on at the moment. You can see that all forty teams are either priority one or two. No priority threes. This means that all teams will be trained in TBT ways of working by

December this year. And we'll have completed E2Es on our twenty core processes by July the following year.'

Take PTM snapshots as an audit trail. Whatever you decide what to work on and at what pace, people will challenge it down the line. 'Why did you decide to work on service, why not sales?' That's fine. It's a healthy challenge. The trick is to keep monthly snapshots of your PTM as an audit trail. 'Colleagues, here is a copy of our PTM from last August. It shows why, based on everything we knew at the time, we decided to prioritise service.'

Use the process and teams connections. The PTM connects teams and processes. It shows you at a glance which teams are involved in which processes. This is helpful for your decision making. For example, you might decide to make the E2E sales process and every team involved in the sales process a priority one. This will improve the entire sales system. It has a double whammy benefit. Teams have a streamlined process to work with. And the process is being continually improved by the teams involved.

Another scenario is to look for teams that are involved in many processes. For example, finance teams are often involved in many non-finance processes; not just finance-specific ones. For this reason, up-skilling finance teams in TBT ways of working can positively impact many aspects of the business in addition to finance.

Feel free to use a spreadsheet. I know I said that everything in 3D can be done on a whiteboard. And it can. But rules are there to be broken and if there's one place where a spreadsheet helps it's with the PTM. You can download a PTM Excel template from **the3dworkplace.com** to help get started.

4. Making it real

This case study shows how the PTM tool helped steer a global improvement initiative for a leading consumer products company.

The first version of the PTM was done in an afternoon using Post-it notes on a long office wall.

Altogether, there were forty E2E processes and sixty teams marked up on the PTM. Eight processes were decided as priority one, ten as priority two and the remaining twenty-two as priority three. The CFO decided that the right scale and speed of progress was about twelve E2E processes per year together with TBT training for the teams involved. Anything faster would not be digestible. Anything slower would not have sufficient impact and momentum. This meant that all the priority one and two E2E processes, and the teams involved, would be touched by the initiative in the first year and a half. That felt about right in terms of pace and momentum.

The discussion was kept at a high level. We just needed the first draft to get the right conversations underway. Was the first version absolutely right? No. Did it have ambiguities? Yes. Was it missing things? Yes. Did any of that matter? No. The PTM had done its job in getting agreement on the high priority improvements and the required pace and momentum to impact strategic goals.

4. How do we embed a culture of continuous improvement?

What do we mean by culture? There are many definitions. I like this one: *'Culture is the character and personality of your organisation. It's what makes your business unique and is the sum of its values, traditions, beliefs, interactions, behaviours, and attitudes.'* (ERC. 2019, February)[1]

Organisations with great cultures don't get there by accident. They define the culture they want and then they relentlessly make the decisions and take the actions to create it. They want to create a culture that will support – not undermine – their strategy and objectives. It's not a one-off job. It never stops. It's a constant creation. Creating and sustaining a supportive culture is not fluffy. It's not a few walls covered with clichéd slogans. Or a trendy space with bean bags. It's conscious, deliberate and it's reflected in every element of the organisation. It translates directly into policies, processes, procedures, organisation, governance and technology.

A culture of continuous improvement does not exist in its own separate space. It is part of the overall organisation culture. This is where 3D can play a positive role in influencing your organisation culture. It gives and it takes. Yin and yang. 3D both needs a supportive culture and helps create and sustain that same culture. An analogy might be trees in a forest. They need a culture of rich earth, rain, sunlight and wildlife. They help sustain that same culture by turning carbon dioxide into oxygen, by dropping leaves that decompose to earth and by providing a habitat for a multitude of insects, birds and animals.

Let's go back to our definition of culture and see how 3D helps nourish and sustain each of the six elements: beliefs, behaviours, interactions, attitudes, values and traditions.

Beliefs. Deciding to deploy 3D is a statement of belief that continuous improvement is important. That having streamlined processes is important. That the way teams work and how much people enjoy their work is important. That up-skilling people in effective ways of working is important. It's not talking about beliefs. It's acting on beliefs.

Behaviours. I'm a great believer in changing behaviours by just doing. Not thinking, analysing, talking. Just doing. And then a wonderful thing happens. All sorts of learnings and developments I'd never have imagined start coming out. What sort of behaviours does 3D impact? Here is a quick brain dump: How people communicate at the start of each day. How people prioritise their work. How people perceive their customers and act on their perceptions. How people do their work in practice. How people collaborate to solve problems. How people in different functions engage to streamline work between them. How leaders find out what is actually happening on the ground. Do they sit in an ivory tower reading reports or do they go and see for themselves? We've all heard the phrase: 'Work smarter not harder.' Too often it's just talk. 3D gives you a way to walk the talk.

The manager of a power station was an inspirational leader and insisted on operational excellence as a way of working. He led from the front and demonstrated the behaviours that he expected from his team. Two behaviours in particular helped define the culture.

- Applying workplace organisation tools such as Five S to every part of the environment. He'd asked for our help in expanding it from plant and machinery into the back-office environment. To filing systems, document storage and computer hard drive organisation. So that

every engineer had the same standard ways and could immediately locate the right documents in a colleague's system.

- Go see for yourself. He was rarely in his office. His day was spent walking around the plant. By immersing himself in the environment of an issue, he felt far more equipped to not only help solve the issue at hand, but to also support his team in their own problem-solving ability. And he expected the same from his team.

Interactions. 3D changes how people interact. It replaces finger pointing and the blame game with a standard way to fix things. It replaces 'Who's to blame for this?' with 'There's a problem here. sales, service and credit are all involved. Let's get together and do an A3 to fix it.' 3D changes interactions between people at all levels. Joining a daily huddle is a great way for a leader to meet colleagues and find out what's really happening. It's easier and more natural for everyone concerned. Randomly going up to a team and asking them how it's going can be both awkward and intrusive. Organising formal catch-up meetings can be stilted and – well – a bit formal. Daily huddles also make it easy for team leaders to see what's happening in their peers' teams. 3D breaks down barriers and increases the number and quality of interactions between levels and functions of an organisation.

Attitudes. One definition of attitude is: *'A way of feeling or acting toward a person, thing or situation.'* (YourDictionary, 2022). 3D is a practical way to change from a can't-do to a can-do attitude. From 'it's impossible to change anything around here' to 'it's easy to change things around here. In fact it's expected as part of the job.' From 'everything has to be a project to get improved. And that takes months just to get a go-ahead!' to 'I'll start an A3 next week with John from sales and Anne from operations to get this fixed.' From 'we need highly skilled specialists to improve things' to 'we all have the skills to improve things. The new capacity balancing chart I've introduced to our team performance board is working a treat.'

Values. 3D supports an organisation's values. It helps walk the talk. For example, collaboration is a much stated company value. The problem is that it often doesn't happen in practice. An oft-heard complaint is: 'It's impossible to get anything fixed around here. Everyone just focuses on their own area.' The interesting thing is that everyone usually wants the situation to improve. There isn't a secret gang of uncollaborative people going around putting spikes in wheels! It's just one of those stuck situations.

The organisation had a stated goal to make 'collaboration' one of its core values. Particularly in how people reached out to each other to help fix problems. They created a table of three types of problem and how to use 3D tools to collaborate to fix them. The types of problem were: Within The Team; Between Teams; and Across Functions. The CEO used her townhall all-staff events to communicate the message across the organisation: 'We all want to collaborate. We all want to improve things that we know are wrong and hold us back. Now we have a standard way to do it. We've removed our excuses!'

Traditions. One definition of tradition is: *'A custom or belief that is passed down through the generations or that is done time after time or year after year.'* (YourDictionary 2022). Examples are the Muslim tradition of breaking fast with dates, the Indian tradition of lamps and fireworks at Diwali and the Christian tradition of giving gifts at Christmas.

I was running LCS Level 1c accreditation reviews with eight team leaders for a beverages company. Each leader had made significant improvements in their area using TBT ways of working. It was a fulfilling and enjoyable day listening to each person tell their story. I find the passion, creativity and commitment that people bring to their improvements is inspiring. It is a favourite part of my job!

The plan was to have an accreditation ceremony at 5 pm to award their LCS Level 1c certificates. Someone mentioned that the Global

Leadership Team (GLT) was meeting that same day in the same building. It was unusual to have everyone in the same location and I suggested that we ask the GLT if they would like to attend. And they did. Photographs were taken and a team shot of the eight team leaders holding their certificates together with the GLT ended up on the intranet. It sent a powerful message. It was a chance event but it created a mini tradition. From then on, all LCS certification events were attended by any GLT members in the same location.

We started off this chapter with the following definition of culture: 'Culture is the character and personality of your organisation. It's what makes your business unique and is the sum of its values, traditions, beliefs, interactions, behaviours, and attitudes.' We've seen how 3D both supports and contributes to each of these six elements.

5. What is our 3D Centre?

Any initiative requires leadership and a centre of gravity to get it going and keep it stable. 3D is no different. A simple way is to set up what I call the 3D Centre.

The 3D Centre can take many shapes and sizes. In small organisations, it can be part of someone's job. In medium-sized organisations it might be one, two or three people. In large organisations it can be five people or more. Another way to think of the centre is as the keel on a sailing boat. It keeps the boat stable and on course. Without its keel, the boat would flip over and sink at the first squall.

1. 3D Centre responsibilities

What does the 3D Centre do? Here are some of its main responsibilities:

- **Planning.** Engaging with colleagues across the organisation to prioritise and schedule what to work on and the plan for the future. See section: **AAA Q3: Are we working on the right things at the right pace?**

- **Supporting initiatives.** Being the go-to source of 3D expertise. Joining teams as needed to help their improvement initiatives. Providing light touch governance and updates to leadership. Harvesting and sharing initiative outcomes.

- **Capability building.** Driving the capability building plan for the organisation. Giving the training courses and making training materials available across the organisation. Facilitating the LCS accreditation panels.

- Communicating. Sharing goals, plans, successes and benefits as they come in. Emphasising resilience: 'This is what we are going to do. Yes there will be setbacks. Yes they'll be some failures. Good! We'll learn from the lessons.'

- Going the extra mile. Nothing stands still. The 3D Centre is the lighthouse for continuously improving. Helping colleagues assess how they are doing today and what they want to do better tomorrow. Innovating the 3D approach. Setting new challenges to the organisation.

2. Principles for an effective 3D Centre

There are some helpful principles to follow when setting up your 3D Centre.

Value expertise. Ensure that everyone involved in the centre becomes a hands-on 3D practitioner. Be wary of passengers preparing reports but not getting stuck in. A good rule of thumb is ninety per cent of effort should be on improving things. Ten per cent on reporting and administration. Not the other way round!

Stay lean! Keep the centre small, light touch and under-engineered. Make it a carbon-fibre centre. As light as possible to do the job. Keep the 3D approach simple and pragmatic. There's a natural tendency to over-engineer as time goes on. People like to add things but don't take them away. Methods become like barnacles on a ship's bottom. What started out as a clean slick copper bottom gliding through the water becomes heavy, waterlogged and riddled with barnacles. OK I got carried away on the barnacles bit, but you know what I mean.

Go-see. Tell your colleagues to go and see the work on the ground to find out how it's going. Want to know how the customer service

TBT is going? Join their morning huddle tomorrow. Want to get an update on the sales process E2E? Ask the team to talk you through their value stream map on the wall. A helpful tip: Whatever you say at the beginning becomes the norm. People will accept almost anything at the beginning of an initiative; but not as a change part way though. So if you say right at the outset that go-see is the way to get updates then people will embrace the approach. But if you deliver beautifully engineered PowerPoint decks for the first three months and then announce: 'No more PowerPoint – it's go-see from now on', then fasten your seat belt and expect some turbulence!

Continually improve the approach. It doesn't matter how good something is; we like new things. If the approach doesn't keep improving then there's a risk that people will say after a year or two: 'This is getting a bit boring. I think it's time for something new!' As often as not, the baby gets thrown out with the bathwater. The answer is to establish your improvement approach as a strong brand within your organisation. And to make sure it stays a strong brand by continually improving it. 3D is specifically designed to be own-branded. Most organisations that use 3D have own-branded it with a name and design that resonates with their people and culture. It's the same power and capability under the hood but the name, colours, look and feel and terminology is the organisation's.

Keep benefit tracking simple. This is a personal view having seen every variation of benefit tracking. From the very simple to the incredibly complex. Remember the goal is to improve things not to drown in over-engineered benefits management. One approach is to simply record a list of bullet point benefits for each initiative. A good order is:

•   customer impact

•   staff impact

- revenue growth

- operating performance

- cost reduction

What does this order say? That this initiative is about our customers and our people. When we keep taking the waste out, when we keep flowing more value faster and for less resource, then revenues will grow and costs will fall as an outcome.

3. Making it real

This case study is a good example of a highly effective 3D Centre in action. They called their 3D Centre the OpEx team and their approach was branded 'The OpEx Way'.

The leader of the OpEx team was an inspiring leader. She was highly driven and always pushing for the extra mile. We were supporting her team to roll out The OpEx Way across a wide variety of departments. A few focus areas were asset management, procurement, health and safety, operations and storage. The approach flexed to both asset and service-based areas.

At the end of the initial roll-out phase, and once a quarter thereafter, the business colleagues and the OpEx team jointly completed an OpEx maturity assessment. This comprised answering thirty questions and measuring the success of the OpEx roll-out, highlighting any gaps and refining the continuous improvement plan. The OpEx assessment was regularly completed by all departments in the company and provided a common language and standard. This also helped with E2E process improvements involving several departments.

The leadership team saw a continual stream of benefits and positive feedback from the initiative. They monitored the quarterly team assessments with just one rule: keep improving! Whatever your score was last time, improve on it this time. Simple, highly effective – and always going for the extra mile!

Benefits of Again-and-Again

Benefits of Again-and-Again

There are three main benefits of the AAA dimension. Sustainability, scale of impact and skills development. Let's look at each.

Embedding sustainability. The bedrock benefit of the whole 3D approach. Without sustainability, it's another initiative that did some good for a bit and then fizzled out. AAA is designed to get you to a place where 'it's just the way we do things around here'. And then to stay in that place with a positive paranoia where sustainability is always front of mind. Never taken for granted. Continually nourished. Does AAA guarantee sustainability? No, of course not. What it does is to load the dice in your favour. We've all heard the complaint: 'It's so difficult to change things around here. People are so stuck in their ways.' AAA looks to turn that from a complaint to a virtue. Where TBT ways of working and E2E process performance are so deeply embedded into the culture of the organisation that they're impossible to change!

Delivering scale of impact. Achieving a scale and pace that makes a real difference to your organisation. This can take many forms. It might be mandating the use of A3s. One simple tool that touches everyone in the organisation. It might be agreeing that all teams will design and adopt their own morning huddle. A small change that can have a huge impact.

A gourmet fast food chain with over five hundred outlets worldwide adopts this practice. I'm an early riser and get my early morning coffee there at 7 am. This is the time their team starts so I overhear many

241

Benefits of Again-and-Again

of their huddles. It is fascinating. 'Team, what caused the shortage of lettuce yesterday? Erika, I noticed you struggling with complicated coffee orders. How can I help? There's a big conference down the road today so we can expect a surge of customers at 12.30 pm.'

Notice that scale of impact isn't all about big projects. There is no project in the above case study. It's a behaviour embedded into culture that has a huge impact every day on every customer and front-line work colleague. AAA drives the scale of impact you want to achieve by asking the right questions.

Developing new skills. Hopefully that includes everyone in the organisation. Each of the AAA Five Checklist Questions influences skills development. Leadership learning new skills and behaviours in Question One. Committing to a skills development plan in Question Two. Developing prioritising and actioning skills in Question Three. Building cultural awareness skills in Question Four. And codifying and propagating these new skills through your 3D Centre in Question Five.

The three benefits of AAA mutually support and reinforce each other. Sustainability provides the time duration to achieve the desired scale of impact and to develop new skills across your organisation. Scale of impact reinforces sustainability and promotes learning across the organisation. Developing and then using new skills each day are what makes sustainability real and drives scale of impact.

---

1 ERC. (2019, February). Workplace Culture: What It Is, Why It Matters, and How to Define It. Yourerc.Com. https://www.yourerc.com/blog/post/workplace-culture-what-it-is-why-it-matters-how-to-define-it

Part Six

GETTING STARTED – LET'S GO!

The secret of getting ahead is getting started

- Mark Twain

Getting started overview

There are broadly four ways to get started and any number of variations in between. Each has its advantages depending on what you want to achieve. The four ways are:

- **Starting with Team-by-Team**

- **Starting with End-to-End**

- **Starting with Again-and-Again**

- **Starting in combination**

The following sections look at each in turn with case studies to show how different organisations got started in the way that best suited their environment and objectives.

Starting with Team-by-Team

Starting with TBT is the most usual way to get started. It has a number of advantages. It's fast and straightforward; shows immediate results; focuses on culture and capability building from the start and supports sustainability. It's a new way of working day to day; not a project. It's flexible and easy to refine the approach to your environment. Here are some typical ways to get started with TBT.

1. Team-by-Team roll-out

This is the default approach. Simply agree the teams in scope and work through the TBT Five Questions Checklist with each team. See the section: **Team-by-Team Five Questions Checklist**. It normally takes a team between two to four weeks to work through and implement the checklist. When in doubt, take more rather than less time. What's important is for each new way of working to fully sink in and become a habit. Saving a week here or a week there doesn't matter.

A retail company decided to roll out TBT ways of working to their shared services operation in Poland. There were two hundred and eighty colleagues operating across twenty-one teams. The teams covered HR, finance, operations and IT support. Previous attempts to up-skill the teams in better ways of working had failed because they were project-based. Everything was a project! The team leaders and their teams were already maxed out dealing with ever increasing workloads. Teams often worked late into the evening to get the work finished. The last thing they wanted was another project taking resources away from the teams' normal day-to-day activities.

Four 3D coaches were brought in to work with and up-skill the teams over a period of three months. Each team was given a large whiteboard. Either physical or virtual. The starting point for each team was a morning huddle around their new visual display boards. Each team designed their own visual layout with a common theme to include their customer(s), what they wanted and how success was measured on a daily and weekly basis.

The teams could decide the pace that they started using the other TBT tools such as capacity balancing and A3 problem solving. Some teams moved very quickly and started using all the main TBT tools within the first few weeks. Others moved more slowly. It didn't matter. Feedback from team leaders was positive. The new way of working provided a better service to their customers and reduced stress and late working hours.

In this next case study, the organisation started with TBT, unified with AAA and with a solid foundation in place launched a series of E2Es.

A business-to-business utilities company was constantly fighting fires. One minute debt collection had stalled. The next minute bills were going out late and building up exponential backlogs. Then, at certain times of the year, all customer contracts across the industry came up for renewal at the same time and everyone was battling for business. The sales teams had frenetic activity to retain existing and win new customers during these periods.

Yet when you walked onto the operational floors it felt strangely flat. There was no real sense of urgency or community. Each team was heads-down doing its own thing. Problems, and there were lots, were ignored, worked around or 'it's their fault'. It was clear that the first priority was for the teams to start working effectively. Eight teams in operations and sales were engaged and upskilled with a TBT way of working that they liked and worked in their environment. The goal was to start to drive improvements at a team and inter-team level and to increase the overall baseline capability.

The focus then moved to AAA sustainability by creating a 3D Centre and launching a leadership coaching programme. The priority was embedding better day-to-day operational management. When this was underway the 3D Centre worked with teams across the business to improve E2E processes.

One year on and the change was profound. When you walked onto the floor you could feel a hum of activity. Net debt was down to the lowest levels in three years, the sales team had their best ever seasonal sales round, and a new hub area had been built that had all operational data up on a wall and where all leaders met daily to discuss performance and ways to improve. In this case, the different parts of 3D had been rolled out one after another, each building on the previous dimension.

2. Leading with a particular tool

Some organisations prefer to focus on one TBT tool and let the new ways of working flow through the organisation simply from the use of this one tool.

A good example is making A3s the standard approach to problem solving. The advantage of this approach is its simplicity combined with its depth and where it eventually leads. It's simple because it is just one thing to focus on. It's deep because A3 problem solving brings so many other positive factors into play. Customer purpose. Defining the problem. Engaging stakeholders. Clarity about what good looks like. Measuring performance. Taking action and implementing solutions.

Following on from the previous case study, the same utilities company had a large backlog of unbilled customers. Over one thousand customers, two and a half million revenue and growing bigger every day. These were customers where, for one reason or another, the company was not able to get the necessary information together to send an accurate bill to the customer. This caused problems on many levels. Customers wanted an accurate timely bill so they could pay it on time and avoid nasty surprises down the road. The longer a bill was delayed, the worse the problem got. More time meant more complexity and knots to unravel. More resource and costs by colleagues on total non-value-add work. Ultimately – if the customer was not billed for more than a year – then the revenue was lost. That was the regulation. The problem literally went over a cliff!

An A3 was launched to address the problem. There were four teams involved in resolving each bill. Metering, Change of Tenancy, Billing and Worklists. The root cause of the problem was that each team prioritised their work in different ways. One team used first in first out. Another team worked on the easy stuff first. Yet it needed a unique combination of activities – in the right sequence – between the four teams to unlock and resolve each bill. The A3 team calculated that, with the current way of working, the probability of achieving this correct combination and sequence was less than one per cent. No wonder there was a problem and it was getting worse.

It was decided to test moving from a functional to a Cell Pod way of working. The Cell Pod would include a member from each team – Metering, Change of Tenancy, Billing and Worklists – located together in their own area. This set-up would allow them to align their work priorities in real-time so that they were each doing exactly the right activities in the right order to resolve each case. With a laser-like focus on maintaining the flow of each case through to completion. No delays. No hand-offs. No waste. No misunderstandings. The test results exceeded all expectations. There was a fivefold increase in throughput. It was expanded to become the standard way of working to clear the unbilled accounts. The backlog melted away in three weeks. This case study has an interesting postscript. It ultimately led to all operational work that involved more than one function being handled in Cell Pods. The A3 had triggered a fundamental reorganisation of the enterprise and how work was done.

Some organisations make the daily huddle the cornerstone of their approach.

A renowned hotel in the UK has made daily team huddles the cornerstone of how they maintain quality, service and customer experience at the highest levels. The hotel is run by a famous French chef and most of the staff are French. It is noted for its service, heritage, food, wine and kitchen garden.

I have stayed there a couple of times and noticed these team huddles going on three times a day: 7 am, 11 am and 4 pm. Naturally I was interested and asked if I could observe. The format was always the same. The team leader and staff met beside a large whiteboard. It was marked up into two vertical sections: EVENTS and RESOLUTIONS. First the team talked through and planned all the relevant events in progress or coming down the line. A team member marked up the EVENTS section of the whiteboard with the staff, food, drink and other logistics plans. Then the team moved onto RESOLUTIONS. An interesting title. It suggests not only listing problems and fixes but also getting at the root causes. Every single problem was listed. A broken lamp in room ten. Faulty internet in room fifteen. A vegetable patch showing signs of disease. Slow check-out service the previous day. Nothing was missed. It was listed on the board and only removed when it was fixed. A standard question was: 'How can we stop this happening again?'

Starting with End-to-End

Starting with E2E is the natural approach when the priority is to fix a specific process. Or set of processes. Normally these are priority processes that have a direct and significant impact on the organisation's performance. In this situation it has clear advantages over other options. It focuses on the priority issues; frequently produces transformational results; and builds a new way of working between the functions involved. From a planning perspective, it can help show the big picture ahead of diving into a particular hot spot. In extreme cases, to avoid improving something that is not needed at all.

Here are two examples where starting with E2E was clearly the right option.

Case study one: Driving strategic priorities. *Remember the consumer goods company developing its Process Team Matrix (PTM) in section:* **Are we working on the right things at the right pace?** *Based on the discussions that the PTM triggered it was agreed that the E2E process of taking orders through to making delivery and receiving the cash was far and away the number one priority. The process drove strategic objectives around customer satisfaction, competitive advantage, cash release and cost reduction.*

The organisation operated in over thirty countries. Eighty per cent of revenue came from four regions and these regions had widely different customer structures and environmental conditions. There were significant performance issues with the order to cash process in three of the four regions. The decision was made to make this the priority focus for the first phase.

It proved a good decision. The process was transformed in the three regions and working capital cash release was measured in the hundreds of millions of dollars.

Case study two: Focusing on big issues. *The COO of a European life and pensions organisation selected three E2E processes to prove the 3D approach. On-boarding new corporate clients. Requests for new systems and services from the business to IT. And the Medium Term Planning process. Each had real issues that were impacting the business and causing friction and stress to the colleagues and areas involved. The three processes were very different from each other. Fixing them was a good stress test for the approach. Things went well and the decision was made to upskill the teams involved in TBT way of working as the next step.*

Starting with Again-and-Again

Starting with AAA is an interesting choice. It's making the decision to embed new capability in your work environment as the first priority. The improvements and benefits are positive by-products of this primary objective. The main advantage of this approach is sustainability. It's saying: 'This is not a project. What really matters is that we establish a continuous improvement culture and a better way of working for the long term. That's why embedding a new capability in our organisation is our first priority.'

The focus is simply on improving things. Not on having to prove that it's worth improving things before doing anything.

Most parents ask their children to keep their room tidy. But what would the parents say if their kids turned around and replied, 'Why should I? Show me the business case? Where are the benefits?' I think we would struggle. Or we'd make something up and then our kids might say: 'Prove it before I do anything.' Then we'd really struggle!

Now let's take an AAA approach. We'd make developing the capability in our kids to keep their rooms tidy the main priority. Maybe we'd teach them 'a place for everything and everything in its place'. We'd make it fun. Turn it into a game. Let them choose a storage system that helps.

We all know that the benefits would start flowing. Easier to get to school on time. Less last-minute stress and bad moods. Pens and papers on hand for homework. Clothes and possessions not going missing. And these benefits might trigger other benefits. Higher marks in exams. Better relationships at home. Learning habits that last a lifetime. Passing these same habits onto their kids.

Could we have proved all these benefits in advance? No way! The time and effort that it would have taken are better spent on just developing the capability.

Here is an example where the organisation decided to lead with the AAA dimension. To build and embed a new improvement capability in the organisation as the primary objective.

A global services company had traditionally taken a project-orientated approach to their improvement initiatives. The focus was on three things: benefits, benefits and benefits. Then one of the leaders decided to take a different approach. It was a bold move. In his own words: 'We have always made benefits the only real priority. While this is logical in theory, we encounter three problems in practice.

- *Firstly, arguing about which project has generated the benefits and who should get the credit has become a cottage industry. What a total waste of time. It causes bad feeling and conflict and adds no value.*

- *Secondly, we don't develop any real and sustainable new capability. It's superficial and skin-deep. There's no culture change in the business. As soon as the improvement team leaves we go backwards.*

- *Thirdly, the promised benefits are usually overstated. This causes yet more bad feeling when they don't happen.'*

He decided to turn the approach on its head. The focus moved to capability building as the main priority. Benefits would flow as an outcome of the new improvement capability. He selected ninety team leaders across the functions in scope. They were based in five locations around the world. Face-to-face training was not realistic. All training was remote by video conference. Each team leader chose their own improvement initiative. The three criteria were do-ability, a maximum ten-week duration and measurable positive impact on the business. At the end of the ten weeks they went through their LCS 1c review and accreditation. This wasn't mandatory but strongly recommended.

Each team leader had a weekly one-hour video call with a 3D coach. There were two 3D coaches assigned to the initiative and each coach trained and supported twenty team leaders in parallel over a ten-week duration. It established a regular drumbeat.

Eighty-two of the ninety team leaders achieved their LCS 1c accreditation. The capability building goals were achieved. That was as expected. The real surprise was that the benefits exceeded the outcomes of the traditional benefits first approach. When his boss saw the results she exclaimed: 'Why didn't we do it this way from the start!'

Starting in combination

Starting with a combination of the three dimensions in parallel is the fastest way to deliver big change fast. It recognises the synergies between the three dimensions. It is making the decision to take advantage of these synergies from the get-go. The main requirement is committed leadership. In effect leadership is saying: 'Look, we've got a lot of change to deliver fast. And we need to deliver it as one team across the organisation. So let's just get going and make it happen.'

The advantages of this approach are: scale and speed of change; resilience from each dimension supporting the other two from the start; and cultural impact from the clarity of message across the organisation. At the same time, there are some factors to consider before taking this approach. It is likely to require a larger upfront investment in time and people resource. And the commitment required is full throttle forward and climbing to thirty-five thousand feet as rapidly as possible. The following case study shows how one organisation – faced with the need for large-scale change fast – used this approach to achieve transformational outcomes.

A large telecommunications company was under pressure. Customers were defecting to new and nimble competitors. Morale was low due to multiple rounds of job cuts and there was a strong command and control leadership culture.

Over the years there had been multiple attempts to try to improve processes and team ways of working. Across the business there were scattered pockets of earlier failed initiatives. The CEO and his managing directors could see something needed to change and we were asked to come in and help.

During a meeting they explained: 'We want to create something that teams want to be part of rather than it being centrally pushed onto them. We need to embed a collective responsibility to make things better. Our front-line teams should feel empowered to make improvements themselves and our leaders need to learn how to release pressure rather than ratchet it up the whole time.'

It was clear that the scale of the challenge required something big and fast. The entire system needed improving! The fact that the urgency was coming from the Board meant we were well set up to go in with a combined 3D approach across the organisation.

We identified the top priority end-to-end customer processes and the teams within them. We then started four things in parallel.

- *Launched TBT for all teams within each customer process to improve ways of working and create an excellent foundation of engaged, motivated team members who could take and run with the E2E improvement initiatives. This also delivered benefits within the first few weeks.*

- *Applied the E2E improvement approach across the selected end-to-end processes. It made a big difference that the improvement teams had gone through TBT, understood the key principles and could immediately run with the Agile test and learn initiatives.*

- *Launched a leaders' coaching programme for all leaders within the end-to-end processes. This up-skilled them in how to support their teams and start to create a new leadership culture that prized empowerment over control.*

- *Built a 3D Centre that brought everything together and created a sustainable, evergreen way of scaling the new ways of working across the organisation.*

Eighteen months later, working hand-in-hand with their 3D Centre team, we had initiated eleven interventions across two thousand five hundred people, twelve hundred colleagues accredited, sixty per cent of leaders through coaching, ninety five million euros of benefits identified and thirty-seven million euros realised and owned by the areas that do the work.

What's the next step?

Thank you for reading this book to this point. Now comes the really exciting part!

'What's the next step?'

Only you and your colleagues know the right answer for your organisation and environment. In fact, there may be multiple right answers. Perhaps you just need to get the boat moving before you can steer her. The good news is that, as we've seen, you have many alternatives. Here are some typical scenarios to consider.

- Dive right in. I love this next step. Start having daily huddles from tomorrow. Launch your first A3. Streamline a core process that will make a big difference to both customers and colleagues.

- Build capability. Make capability building the foundation of your approach and watch the snowball effect. Be amazed at the latent talent that you unleash. And the subsequent impact on your performance and results.

- Take the careful and considered approach. Maybe that's the right way for your people and culture. Give people a copy of this book. See who embraces its principles. Organise a working session. Build consensus on the best way forward. And iterate from there.

- Have a chat with a 3D expert. Go to the next section: **Help and support available**. We would love to talk.

So just take a quiet moment to reflect and ask yourself right now this one question: **'What's MY next step?'**

Help and support available

There is a full range of help and support for 3D to suit you and your environment. This includes:

the3dworkplace.com. This gives you access to helpful downloads, templates and videos. You can subscribe to receive weekly 3D hints and tips. It makes you part of the fast-growing global community of fellow 3D enthusiasts and practitioners.

Expert 3D support. This is available in person on-site or by video call. Our support covers co-leading 3D initiatives, training, capability building and coaching. Every element of 3D has been designed for remote working as well as for more traditional work environments. Please contact **info@the3dworkplace.com** to set up an introductory chat.

3D innovation. 3D is always improving. Some recent innovations include remote working, intelligent automation and process management software.

Thank you!

Thank you for reading this book! We hope that you have taken value from it. And most importantly that you are inspired to get going with 3D in whatever way makes most sense for you and your organisation.

We are confident that you will find the experience and the benefits worthwhile and rewarding. Not only in happier customers, higher revenues and lower costs, but in greater enjoyment of daily working. Enjoying new ways of working with colleagues. Enjoying delighting your customers. Enjoying learning new skills and capabilities.

The purpose of this book has always been a simple one. To make the principles of work working well available to everyone. In any type and size of organisation. And in a way that makes sense because it is common sense. To strip away the mumbo jumbo. To move on from academic arguments about which methods are best to a framework that combines the best of the best.

We wish you well for your journey ahead!

James and Rob
2022

Recommended reading

As you can probably tell by now I'm fascinated by the whole area of making work work better. Here are eighteen of my favourite books including a short note on each one. I've categorised them into four areas:

1. **Fundamentals of Lean thinking.** These will give you a good understanding of the history of Lean and the tools and methods that underpin the thinking.

2. **Application to different areas.** Lean has spread and evolved across many different areas and types of work. Each adaptation has its own characteristics which serve the type of work and also contribute to the whole. These books cover six different areas.

3. **Culture and leadership.** It's not all about tools and methods. These five books are very different but with one thing in common: inspirational in their examples and stories of continuous improvement culture and leadership.

4. **Systems Thinking.** These three books provide a good understanding of systems thinking and its power to effect change.

GETTING STARTED - LET'S GO!

1. Fundamentals, methods and tools

Lean Thinking - Banish Waste and Create Wealth in the Corporation
Jim Womack and Dan Jones. 2003. 2nd edition. London: Simon & Schuster. A seminal work that defined Lean and raised widespread awareness of its potential. Includes a fascinating case study on The Wiremold Corporation and how its CEO Art Byrne and his colleagues, using Lean principles, quadrupled the company size and increased its value by 2,500% in less than 10 years.

The Lean Toolbox - A Handbook for Lean Transformation
John Bicheno and Matthias Holweg. 2016 (5th edition). Buckingham: PICSIE books. A comprehensive guide to Lean tools and methods including easy to understand diagrams and examples. The authors explain both the tools and equally important the thinking and rationale behind them.

Toyota Production System - Beyond Large-Scale Production
Taichii Ohno. 1988. New York: Productivity Press. Taichii Ohno, often called the father of Lean thinking, takes us through - in his personal and unique style - the history of Toyota and his pioneering role in creating The Toyota Production System..

Understanding A3 Thinking - A Critical Component of Toyota's PDCA Management System
Durward K Sobek II and Art Smalley. 2008. Boca Raton FL: CRC Press, Taylor & Francis Group. This book explores layer after layer of A3 thinking including multiples variations of A3s, the psychology behind the approach and the behaviours that it drives. Strongly recommended for anyone considering using A3 thinking.

2. Application to different areas

The Lean Startup - How Constant Innovation Creates Radically Successful Businesses

Eric Ries. 2011. London: Portfolio Penguin. A best seller from a serial entrepreneur who uses Lean principles to power the success of his many startups. The theme of test and learn echoes throughout the book. Highly recommended reading not just for startups but for any new and creative initiative.

Far from the Factory - Lean for the Information Age

George Gonzalez-Rivas and Linus Larsson. 2011. New York: Taylor and Francis Group. Focuses on the use of Lean principles to streamline and remove waste from information flows rather than physical activities. Excellent content on Information Elements (INFELS). A must read book for using Lean in today's information-centric work environment.

Lean Software Development - An Agile Toolkit

Mary and Tom Poppendieck. 2003. Boston: Addison-Wesley. Groundbreaking book on the application of Lean thinking to software development. A great explanation on Lean itself and how Lean principles underpin Agile software development. The first of a series of best-selling books by the Poppendiecks including 'Implementing Lean Software Development - From Concept to Cash.'

The Toyota Product Development System - Integrating People Process and Technology

James M. Morgan and Jeffrey K. Liker. 2006. New York: Productivity Press. How did Toyota get the Prius to market in 18 months against the industry average of 36 months for a new car? A breakthrough product and global bestseller. Morgan and Liker distill it down to 12 principles that can be applied to any type of new product development.

Real Numbers - Management Accounting in a Lean Organisation
Jean E Cunningham and Orest J Fiume with Emily Adams. Durham NC: Managing Times Press. Detailed application of Lean principles and methods to the world of management accounting. A must-read for anyone looking to get a new level of value from their finance function.

A Factory of One - Applying Lean Principles to Banish Waste and Improve Your Personal Performance
Daniel Markovitz. 2011. Boca Raton FL: CRC Press, Taylor and Francis Group. Lean isn't just for organisations and teams. It's for you and me! A fascinating read on how each of us, as individuals, can apply Lean principles to our daily work and activities. So we can focus on the valuable things we love doing, be more productive and have more fun.

3. Lean culture and leadership

Creating a Lean Culture - Tools to Sustain Lean Conversions
David Mann. 2010. New York: Productivity Press. This book focuses on creating the right culture. There used to be a tendency to think of Lean as a bunch of tools and methods. This book challenges that. It has a laser focus on creating the right culture for sustainable continual improvement. Yes, the tools are part of the solution but they are a means to an end rather than an end in themselves.

The Speed of Trust - The One Thing That Changes Everything
Stephen M Covey with Rebecca R. Merrill. 2018. New York: Simon & Schuster Inc. An inspirational book that examines what happens when you remove the toxic waste of distrust and move to a high trust working environment. Clearly it needs to be a trust based on competence and Covey and Merrill provide a clear and practical roadmap on how to achieve and benefit from a 'Speed of Trust' culture and environment.

Better Thinking, Better Results - case study and analysis of an enterprise-wide Lean transformation
Bob Emiliani with David Stec, Lawrence Grasso and James Stodder. 2007 2nd edition: Kensington CT: The Center for Lean Business Management. A first hand view of the Wiremold Corporation Lean transformation told by Bob Emiliani, its Chief Operating Officer. What makes it so special and permeates every page is the 'respect for people' principle that combines with 'continuous improvement' to drive the transformation. I took away three lasting memories: respect for people, respect for people and respect for people.

Turn The Ship Around! A True Story of Building Leaders by Breaking the Rules
L. David Marquet. 2015. New York: Portfolio Penguin Group. David Marquet was the captain of a US nuclear submarine. He achieved extraordinary results by breaking away from command and control, pushing decisions down to the lowest responsible level and providing the training and culture to support. The question "What do you intend to do?" assumes a whole new significance.

Legacy 15 Lessons in Leadership - What the All Blacks Can Teach Us About the Business of Life
James Kerr. 2013. London: Constable. A distillation of 15 leadership principles that underpin the success of one of the most successful teams in the world. More than leadership it's a way of being. Here's the first one to provide a glimpse: *'CHARACTER - Sweep the sheds. Never be too big to do the small things that need to be done.'* Simple yet says it all. A brilliant and fascinating book.

4. Systems Thinking

Thinking in Systems - A Primer
Donella H Meadows. 2009. London: Earthscan. An excellent introduction to Systems Thinking. Clear, concise and packed with examples and diagrams that make it easy-to-understand in theory and how it can be applied to everyday problems.

Out of The Crisis

W. Edwards Deming. 1982. Cambridge MA: Massachusetts Institute of Technology. Deming has been called the father of modern systems thinking. This book calls for a radically different approach to leadership and problem solving. If your first instinct when something goes wrong is: 'Who's to blame?' then read this book. Includes his now-famous quote: *'The system is responsible for 94% of problems.' (Page 315)*

Systems Thinking in the Public Sector - the failure of the reform regime and a manifesto for a better way

John Seddon. 2010. Axminster: Triarchy Press. A hard-hitting critique of the typical targets-led reform approach in the public sector. Seddon proposes a better way using Systems Thinking as the foundation. Packed full of examples from the public sector including the health service, education and policing.

Glossary of terms

I made a promise at the beginning of this book to avoid any jargon or consultancy speak. It's all plain language common-sense. At the same time there are a few terms that I've used where it might be helpful to give a definition.

1. Core 3D terms

Continuous Improvement. The ongoing improvement of products, services or processes through both incremental and breakthrough steps.

Lean. Flowing more value to customers for less resource by the elimination of waste.

Operational Excellence. The execution of work in an excellent way. Given two organisations with the same strategy, the operationally more excellent company will in general have better operational results, creating value for customers and stakeholders.

Systems Thinking. A holistic approach to analysis that focuses on the way that a system's constituent parts interrelate and how systems work over time and within the context of larger systems.

2. Related terms and abbreviations

Key Performance Indicators (KPI). Critical (key) indicators of progress toward an intended result. KPIs provide a focus for strategic and operational improvement, create an analytical basis for decision making and help focus attention on what matters most.

Remote Working. A working style that allows people to work outside of a traditional office environment. It is based on the concept that work does not need to be done in a specific place to be executed successfully. This has become a widely accepted way of working since Covid 19.

Service-Level Agreement (SLA). A commitment between a service provider and a client. Particular aspects of the service – quality, availability, responsibilities – are agreed between the service provider and the service user.

Standard Operating Procedure (SOP). A set of step-by-step instructions compiled by an organisation to help the people doing the work carry out routine operations. SOPs aim to achieve efficiency, quality output and uniformity of performance, while reducing miscommunication and failure to comply with regulations.

3. Capabilities that can leverage 3D

Artificial Intelligence (AI). The ability of a machine to display human-like capabilities such as reasoning, learning, planning and creativity. AI enables technical systems to perceive their environment, deal with what they perceive, solve problems and act to achieve a specific goal.

Data Analysis. The process of inspecting, cleansing, transforming, and modelling data with the goal of discovering useful information, informing conclusions, and supporting decision-making.

Digitalisation. Enabling or improving processes by leveraging digital technologies and digitised data.

Robotic Process Automation (RPA). Automating basic tasks through software or hardware systems that function across a variety of applications, just as human workers do. RPA software is designed to reduce the burden for employees of completing repetitive, simple tasks.

About James and Rob

James Lascelles

Twenty-one years ago I read my first book on making work work better. Achieving more for less by focusing on value to customers and removing waste. I was hooked! Not just in a rational way but at a gut level. It resonated with my personal belief of the need to take good care of resources. I decided that this would be my life's career, passion and mission.

I led my first improvement initiative in 2001. Then my second, then my third... until by my current count I've led about fifty initiatives. Some global. Some much smaller. Through the journey I've learnt a bit about what works and, just as importantly, what doesn't.

After a spell with one of the big five consultancies and then with a global services organisation I was fortunate to join Baringa Partners LLP. My job was to build the process excellence practice. One of the first people to join me was Rob Maguire with whom I'd worked many years earlier. Eight years later our team had grown to seventy people. The most inspiring group of people I have ever worked with. Early on in our Baringa journey we developed the 3D framework. A way of combining the best of the best operational excellence thinking, concepts, tools – call it what you will – into a common-sense framework that people can immediately relate to.

3D has been in continual development ever since and is now used by organisations of every size and sector worldwide. That's good but there's one thing that has always bothered me. Whenever I explain what I do most people have no idea what I'm talking about. There is a general lack of awareness of the basic principles of making work work better. They're too specialist, too dry and boring. But actually they're not. These principles are fascinating and can benefit any work environment. In days, not weeks or months.

So I decided to write a book that would reveal all and make the fundamentals of work working better available to everyone. In a way that is quick and easy to read and, most important of all, to apply. That's the purpose of this book. I hope you find it rewarding and motivating and reap the benefits of The 3D Workplace that these fundamentals unleash.

James

London 2022

Rob Maguire

Not many people can say they were destined from childhood to be an operations improvement consultant! Even as a young boy I was intent on making things work better, from toys to games to school work.

Fast forward several decades and I have spent my life understanding how different organisations work to help them operate more effectively and bring about lasting change. For me, it's the people closest to the customer who hold the key to how a business works and can drive the improvements, transforming the work experience for the leadership teams, the clients and most importantly the colleagues themselves.

James and I met when I was starting out as a consultant and over the years he has been my closest advisor, mentor and good friend. The amazing team we have built together at Baringa Partners LLP, the 3D framework, which has been at the core of what we do, and the many client experiences that have shaped us, have made this book what it is.

We hope that everyone who embraces its simple principles finds that their time at work becomes that bit more purposeful, productive and satisfying. We wish you every success.

Rob

London 2022

Lightning Source UK Ltd.
Milton Keynes UK
UKHW022102211122
412610UK00020B/296/J